The
Purple
Parachute

*A Woman's Guide to Navigating
the Winds of Career Change*

PAULA BATTALIA BRAND

The Purple Parachute / Paula Brand — 1st ed.

ISBN Paperback 979-8-9866896-4-7

ISBN Hardcover 979-8-9866896-5-4

ADVANCED PRAISE FOR *THE PURPLE PARACHUTE*

"This compact and complete career guide could easily be titled "The Busy Woman's Guide to Career Success." It offers up-to-the-minute advice on every aspect of career management, with emphasis on the unique challenges that women face in the job hunt and in the workplace."

KAREN JAMES CHOPRA, LPC, CCC, NCC author of *Coaching Career Clients Through Salary and Other Workplace Negotiations*

"From the first page, Paula Brand writes extremely compelling and timely guidance for every woman wanting to explore options in today's professional world. As a clinical career counselor and coach, I have written and read countless books, websites, and blogs aimed to help people in career and life transition. Paula's book is truly a must-read for anyone who wants straightforward advice with a clear path forward. This book helps you navigate career questions from a trusted and highly experienced professional.

Paula weaves practical guidance with her personal story, and with unique and insightful words of wisdom, every reader will feel lucky to spend hours with Paula just by diving into her book."

ILANA TOLPIN LEVITT, mental health counselor, clinical career counselor, and author of *What's Mom Still Got to Do With It?*

"Written by a woman for women, *The Purple Parachute* provides the process needed in today's post-COVID world to secure employment. Paula Brand has compiled assessments and activities to help every woman discover her own uniqueness and priorities to guide her toward the best career options.

No one said that securing a new job would be easy, but with this resource, women looking for a new job will find everything they need to put their best foot forward as they pursue a new job.

It's a must-read for every woman of any age."

HANNAH MORGAN, job search strategist, founder of Career Sherpa.net, and author of *The Infographic Resume*

"I can say from first-hand experience that my career benefited from the A.S.T.E.R. Career Model shared in *The Purple Parachute*. Although I am a high achiever and a fast learner, I could not figure out what job direction I wanted. I was trying to do too many things in the wrong order and was just a mess.

I'm delighted that Paula has written *The Purple Parachute* to help other women in their careers. After reading it and living through the process, I can assure you that the A.S.T.E.R. Career Model works."

LAURIE NEDERVEEN, director of program development in the human service industry

"Paula Brand puts her extensive experience as a leading career counselor to work in *The Purple Parachute*. This book brims with stories of how the women she coached found fulfilling work. Chapters include a variety of exercises and strategies for women who are ready to take a thoughtful approach to re-tooling their careers. From questionnaires to skills analysis, and a personality assessment, this book provides readers with ways to gather the insight and knowledge essential to a successful career transition."

MAGGIE ROGERS, instructional designer

"It is such an honor and privilege to share a few words about *The Purple Parachute* by Paula Brand. She provides practical tools to help job seekers and career changers uncover "what's next" for the upcoming chapter of their professional lives. The gift of *The Purple Parachute* is empowering job seekers—especially women—to use the A.S.T.E.R. Career Model to reassess where they are, to redesign their personal and professional mission and vision, as they reconnect with their core values of their WHOLE SELVES while moving toward "what's next." I love how Paula shares stories to highlight each facet of the career changers' process in uncovering that "something inside so strong" (Labi Siffre), which compels us to become the right person who is ready for the right opportunity at the right time in the right space. I cannot wait to share these tools with some of my career-exploration students as they map out the immediate and short-distant futures of their lives."

KARLA M. WYNN, emerging business owner and higher education professional specializing in academic, career and workforce development services at Harford and Anne Arundel Community Colleges

AUTHOR'S NOTES

The title of this book is an ode to Richard Bolles and his globally influential book *What Color is Your Parachute?* His book had a profound influence on my life, and I was lucky enough to meet him a few times before he passed away. His legacy is never ending.

The title was also inspired by the poem "Warning" by Jenny Joseph that has a famous opening line: "When I am an old woman I shall wear purple...." This poem reminds me of the courage of women and the boldness that a mature woman grows into with time. These qualities can help us work through career transitions.

For confidentiality purposes, I intentionally changed the names of people in the illustrative stories provided throughout the book. Similarly, in sharing my story, I left out specific names of organizations and people.

CONTENTS

"Just don't give up on trying to do what you really want to do. Where there is love and inspiration, I don't think you can go wrong."

ELLA FITZGERALD

The World Of Work Today

The workplace is not what it used to be

The world of work is relentlessly changing. It's now officially a gig economy and no employment situation is entirely secure. Many employees have begun a side business or quit to go all in with entrepreneurship. Many employers look for loyalty, though many are not willing to give it.

And all of that happened before the COVID-19 pandemic and recent social movements. Those events added additional changes to our workplaces. They offered some positives, such as normalizing remote work, questioning privilege, forcing innovation, and requiring more accountability for diverse workplaces. At the same time, there have been many downsides. Entire industries were crushed by COVID-19. Directly and indirectly, an already tough labor market has been exacerbated. Most employers have found trouble filling roles and many professionals are choosing to leave their field—in some cases dropping out of the workforce altogether.

For women, there are specific challenges from COVID-19, including work-life balance and safety issues. Many mothers had to choose between work or family. Many women quit work during COVID-19 so they could be more available for their families. For those who continued to work, family responsibilities became more challenging. Before COVID-19, women consistently handled more household work than men. After COVID-19, that trend only intensified. In terms of safety, sexual harassment didn't stop when work went virtual; it only lessened inappropriate in-person actions. Domestic violence increased and women were more often in the role of the victim. This rise is not surprising considering that COVID-19 created stressful situations and forced people to live in close quarters for extended periods of time.

Women who are savvy know that transition is a reality in many stages of their career and embrace a "portfolio career." In case you haven't heard that term before, let me explain. There are two major aspects to a portfolio career. First, it allows for one professional to implement multiple talents and interests in different ways. Secondly, it encourages a myriad of income streams so that if one dries up, another can sustain during transitions. A portfolio career can be developed over time. An example would be someone who is a professional working full time in one profession and has a part-time consulting business on the side (separate or related to the full-time work). This person can also be paid to speak to groups and may have other platforms, such as a blog, a book, or an online course.

The new workplace has many analogies, but the one that resonates the most for me is that of a movie set. I first heard this analogy in the closing keynote by Mark Savickas at the 100th anniversary conference of the National Career Development Association (keynote, NCDA annual conference, Boston, MA, July, 10, 2013). Jobs have become project-based and employers are increasing their use of contractors and temporary teams to complete assignments as needed. Just like a movie set, people come together to complete a time-specific project and then part ways.

The current economic realities have reached the point where every person must take ownership of her own career management journey. Employers can no longer be expected to direct this aspect of your life. Personally, I think that's a good thing. It can seem scary at first, but, ultimately, having control over your career creates more variety and opportunities for you to grow. I've learned from many years of practicing career advising with women from all around the world that career management is not common sense to most people. We haven't been taught about it in our early years or at least not much beyond Career Day. Many college students have never accessed their career center office, and career management has never been a major part of formal schooling at any stage of adult life. However, just because it's not ingrained in our culture it doesn't mean it's hard to do. With some guidance and some effort, you can easily take control of your career and see positive results.

All of this change and the need to drive your career is happening to everyone in the workplace, but some populations are feeling it more than others. As one segment of the workforce, women have their own unique workplace and career issues (the glass ceiling, unequal pay, balancing caregiving and working, to name a few), which is why it's even more important for women to take charge of their own careers to increase their chance of finding job satisfaction and to create their own career freedom.

This book is designed to empower women to do just that! It will help you take ownership of your career using a career cycle model that is useful any time you are experiencing a career transition or in preparation for a future change in your work. For mid-career women, this may happen quite often. So, it's a good idea to learn about this model, not just for now, but also for your future career management.

My story

I will share more of my story throughout this book where it is relevant, but let's start with how I realized that it's up to you to take charge of your career. I learned, from my first salaried position in the 90s, that no job is guaranteed even if I'm doing it well. I was let go after a year and a half of dedicated service to a non-profit running programs to help people with developmental disabilities. During my time there, I wrote grants and applied for funding opportunities that sustained the program I ran. My efforts rewarded the organization with approximately $100,000 worth of grant funding and acceptance as a V.I.S.T.A. Volunteer Service Site, which provided four full-time volunteer positions, growing the center further. Unfortunately, all of this was to no avail. In due time, I was let go by the organization because it was not financially in good shape. That was the first time I lost a job due to no fault of my own, but it wouldn't be the last.

In 2009, I was fired for the first and only time in my life. There was no good reason for letting me go, nor was I given one (my former boss later apologized and wrote me a recommendation). Once again, I had been doing everything the company asked me and more. I was devastated by this event. It really shook my confidence and took a lot of time to heal.

I had lost what I thought was my dream job, which was a mortifying experience. Out of the blue, my boss and the head of human resources invited me into a meeting. They gave me the opportunity to resign (with the understanding that if I did not choose that, I would be fired). I knew resigning was smarter, so I took that route. It helped me preserve a tiny piece of dignity, but I knew the company fired me in my heart and mind. As was normal protocol for this employer, they asked me to pack up all of my belongings on the spot, and I was escorted from the building by security.

I remember my dad consoling me: "Paula, everyone has to get fired once in their life." Others shared the perspective of an upside that I realized is very true. Ultimately, it has made me a better career advisor because I lived through this experience.

Along the way, despite these unanticipated setbacks, I realized that I developed a series of talents and transferable skills. After a substantial career path that transitioned my career from education to human resources, then HR to real estate, then real estate to workforce development and, finally, finding my true calling with career advising, I understood that the landscape of the workforce was changing. I could see the wisdom behind the cliché advice that "multiple sources of income" in a career setting meant not being too dependent on any employer. I embraced the idea of building up my "career management insurance" by taking control of my career and diversifying my income streams. I also realized that I uniquely positioned myself to help others take charge of their careers.

In 2011, I started my own business for multiple reasons. First, to create new streams of income beyond one employer. Second, to challenge myself to jump into the pool of entrepreneurship. Third, to find a way to share my talents on my own terms. All three reasons boiled down to taking charge of my livelihood. Thus began my portfolio career. I dipped my foot into entrepreneurship while working full time, so I had a stable income to count on. I wanted a Plan B in case circumstances and my career plans did not align. I didn't know it at the time, but these preparations laid the foundation for the confidence to lay myself off in 2013. (As a lead career advisor, I was tasked with letting one of our team go. I decided it would be me.)

My initial business model focused on resume writing, but I quickly realized that it was not a good fit. That experience also solidified my philosophy that I'd rather teach people career skills they could use for life than create a document for them. I switched my business to focusing on career management and using LinkedIn for adults from all walks of life. Now, I have further zeroed in on those I enjoy helping the most and found my true passion: helping mid-career to executive women succeed in their careers.

As an entrepreneur, I have truly enjoyed my experience so far. While it's certainly a challenge, especially with creating a stable income, I have been afforded flexibility in scheduling and travel, which was extremely helpful in the years before my dad passed away. It has taught me to think like a businesswoman in addition to thinking like a career counselor. I can manage my time better, and I can make a direct impact on my income.

My mom's story—it's never too late

My mom is a great inspiration to me in many ways, but especially when it comes to her career journey. After getting married at the age of 18, she had six children. I'm the youngest. She then took on, as a volunteer, many important local, political movements of the time. She returned to school at age 32, finished her bachelor's, and then immediately enrolled in and graduated from law school. She was a three-term elected supervisor (similar to a mayor) of my hometown. In 1986, she ran in a New York congressional primary. In 1990, she created a local non-profit to provide housing to low-income families. She recently retired as a town judge. All the while, she was, and continues to be a very successful self-employed practicing real estate attorney.

My mother unknowingly served as my first career role model and introduced me to the idea of a portfolio career long before that term got coined. Her actions proved to me that it's never too late to begin a career and that determination pays off. She also beautifully illustrates that your career is a journey and only one part of a rich, fulfilling life. It's not a race, so enjoy the process!

It is not unusual for mothers to influence their daughters' career paths. My colleague, Ilana Tolpin Levitt, wrote an excellent book on this topic, titled *What's Mom Still Got to Do With It?* Her book provides a framework helping women examine their relationship with their mothers. This exploration helps women gain insight into their actions and their careers. This book also offers suggestions for addressing potential career barriers resulting from the mother-daughter relationship.

If you are willing to do the necessary work, you can achieve career satisfaction. I've seen clients do it over and over again. It does take effort and discipline, but it's not an unattainable secret. Your hard work will pay off in a more satisfying career path.

THE A.S.T.E.R. CAREER MODEL

I'd like to introduce you to a concept called the A.S.T.E.R. Career Model. Each letter represents a step in the career management process. This book will walk you through each stage and share resources to help you move through each step. It is possible to work through this on your own, but if you find you need additional help, you may need to speak with a career coach. Sometimes working with a career professional may be helpful in two ways: It can make the process happen faster, and it can be advantageous to see things objectively.

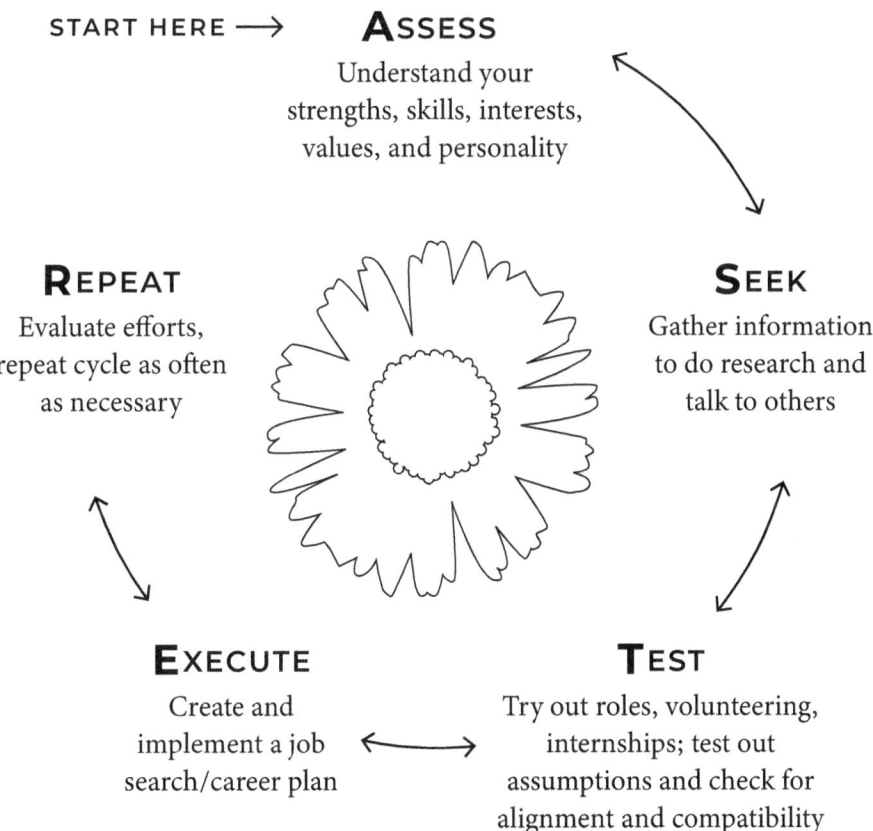

START HERE ⟶ **A**SSESS
Understand your
strengths, skills, interests,
values, and personality

REPEAT
Evaluate efforts,
repeat cycle as often
as necessary

SEEK
Gather information
to do research and
talk to others

EXECUTE
Create and
implement a job
search/career plan

TEST
Try out roles, volunteering,
internships; test out
assumptions and check for
alignment and compatibility

Assess: The book starts here. Assessing yourself is the most important step! It involves reflecting on your V.I.N.E.S. (Values, Interests, Natural Disposition, Exceptional Qualities, and Skills) to determine potential opportunities that might be a good fit for you now or in the future.

Seek: This step involves research—through books, the internet, and speaking with others. This is the first part of your exploration. Narrow down options and rule out jobs/careers as you discover they are not the best fit for you.

Test: Next, you need to test out options. Find opportunities to test your assumptions and continue exploring until you have narrowed them down to a few variable options.

Execute: Whether your goal involves getting a job at a new company, working your way up within your current company, or starting your own business, you need a plan in order to execute it successfully. This section will touch upon each of these paths and offer guidance on how to implement a successful job search.

Repeat: You will likely go through this process multiple times in your career. Once you have initially gone through the A.S.T.E.R. Career Model, the second time may be faster. If things in your life have changed, it's always a good idea to start at the beginning with assessment.

This model is not completely linear or one-directional. It is possible to go back to a previous step if you get stuck along the way. It's also possible to work on two areas simultaneously (such as exploring and testing). The most important thing is to find out where you are in this model and move forward in a direction that gets you closer to where you want to be in your career.

If you already have a very good idea of the next opportunity you want to pursue, you can jump ahead to Chapter Ten Execute Your Career Plan.

If you are seeking to change jobs or re-enter the workforce, you will always have the best chance of top earnings by going for a job where you have past experience. That said, if what you did in the past wasn't satisfying, I suggest you begin with the assessment step.

How to use this book

Perhaps you will want to go through the book as fast as possible, which will be easier if you are not working right now. This process might take some time. If you are not sure what you want to do next, you should definitely work through Part One to go through the self-assessment process and Part Two to flesh out options to consider.

If you already know what you want to do next but are not sure how to get it, Part Three will be most helpful as it focuses on how to land your next satisfying gig. This part covers advice on managing your career, resume development, interviewing, and networking. It's okay to jump around to whichever section is most helpful to you. If you happen to have an interview scheduled, please jump to that part of Chapter 11 right away to help you prepare.

ACTIVITIES

Throughout this book, you'll see places to record information and respond to questions. To get the most out of the information, I encourage you to take time to contemplate them and record your answers. Taking time to reflect is one the most important gifts you can give yourself. This is especially true when making career decisions.

In addition, some chapters feature group activities. I want to emphasize the value of having a support network, which provides accountability and other people's perspectives. If that works for you but you are not part of a group, try to find someone else who is going through a similar career change. Maybe start or join a book club (if you haven't already), and include this book on your reading list. Is there a local job club you could join? (Check your local workforce development office, nearby places of worship, or run a Google search).

SUMMARY

- The world of work is not what it used to be.

- You need to take charge of your career because no one else will ever care about it as much as you!

- I am an experienced, dedicated, and trustworthy professional who has gone through career transitions of my own and learned from them. By sharing this knowledge with you, I hope to guide you so you can pull yourself through any future career transitions.

- If you feel stuck in your career, following the A.S.T.E.R. Career Model can help move your career forward. This book will walk you through this process.

*"The very least you can do in your life
is to figure out what you hope for. And the most
you can do is live inside that hope."*

BARBARA KINGSOLVER

PART ONE

AWARENESS

Discovering Where You Are Right Now

"At the end of the day, you know yourself best."

ABIGAIL JOHNSON

CHAPTER ONE

Assess

The starting point of any career management effort is to know yourself! Learning more about yourself will never be a waste of time. This vital process always involves introspection, reflection, and sometimes career assessment tools. If you already know yourself very well, this part may be easier than you expect. If it's been a while since you've really connected with your inner strengths, it may take more work, but discovering your talents is achievable.

Either way, you need to take some time to think about who you are at your core (your values and strengths) and what you really enjoy (interests and skills). And of course, your personality has an effect on the types of careers that may be a better fit. Though self-assessment is the part most people want to skip or gloss over, you cannot skip this assessment step. I REPEAT, YOU CANNOT SKIP THIS PART! Trust me, the hard work will pay off in a more satisfying career path. This part can even be fun, if you cultivate curiosity.

You may need to repeat this step multiple times in your career journey because the only constant in life is change. Your life and work situations will change, your interests might change, and, as you grow and develop, your talents may shift. Strengths and passions can be developed over time and lead you in a new direction. People get bored, burned out, or find they need a change. All of these situations necessitate career transition.

Those transitions create a series of changes that may seem unrelated, but there is often a career theme that is present over time. If change seems to be taking you on an unusual journey, in hindsight, these voyages often take us where we belong. Seeing these themes and hints as they develop can give you critical clues for possibly new and satisfying directions.

Let me tell you a little bit about my career path, as an example. After my first layoff, I went through the A.S.T.E.R. Career Model. This process led me to apply for and obtain a position working in an HR department running a grant program that trained people for entry level jobs in healthcare. I didn't know it at the time, but there is an entire industry focusing on getting people trained and hired. It's called workforce development, and this grant provided occupational training and job placement opportunities to help women get off of welfare subsidies. The program had down times, so I offered to help in other areas of HR, which exposed me to all facets of HR, and I became an HR generalist.

That job positioned me to take on an HR role running a one-person HR department at a nursing home. I really enjoyed things the first few years but, after handling many aspects of the HR function, I burned out. I was a one-woman HR department for almost 200 employees, handling everything from hiring to compliance. The tipping point occurred when I was assigned the added duty of payroll because numbers are not my strength.

Around the same time, my husband was running a real estate business alone and in need of hiring an employee. I figured nothing could be worse than payroll, so I earned my real estate license, and together we operated a brokerage. After co-managing a successful business for a few years, I realized something profound: While I was fully competent as a realtor, I wasn't passionate about helping people find housing the same way I was about helping people land jobs. I took myself back through the A.S.T.E.R. Career Model again, which brought me back full circle to workforce development, where I stayed for almost 10 years.

In retrospect, I was doing what I loved in my first HR role. Even though the HR department housed the job, it mainly involved running a workforce development program to train welfare recipients for entry level jobs in healthcare. Because I was new to HR and workforce development, I didn't realize the distinction between the two. They are two different sides of the hiring process. A large part of HR is about bringing employees on board and retraining them. Workforce development is about helping people land jobs.

The theme throughout all of my jobs was helping people with a major life goal, (buying a home, getting a job, or deciding on a career path). Financial planners also focus on helping others meet a major life goal, but I should never be one because I dislike working with numbers and math.

Even though life changes constantly, you as a person may or may not. Some people do change. Notably, drastic life events can change people, and physical and mental illnesses can affect personality. However, in most cases, usually by our mid-twenties, we develop some consistency in our personality traits and a solid foundation of our core values. These are guiding points of light that should help you when making important decisions throughout your career.

If you're not so sure about your values, personality, skills, and interests, don't get discouraged. It takes a little effort, but the answers are within you. Trust me. Even though I value the service I provide and am a skilled professional in the field of careers, all the people I have helped had the answers within themselves. I help others gain clarity, but it requires getting in tune with yourself, your strengths, what you value in life, your personality style, what interests you, and where you are most skilled.

Involving and listening to others can be a powerful part of this process. No matter how you gather the information, it is useful to get feedback from people you trust who have your best interests in mind. We can use that feedback to verify information you're collecting about yourself. Keep in mind that everyone has an opinion, so ask and listen to what others share. However, don't neglect listening to yourself. Ultimately, it's your career. Sometimes, others in your life have their own agenda and their opinions can be biased. If you get the same feedback from many people, it's likely accurate. If one person shares something that goes against all other data, view that opinion with some skepticism. Be honest with yourself and see if there is any truth in the comment. But at the end of the day, it's okay to discount an outlier view. The developmental themes you seek will always come up over and over again in different ways. If you listen for the theme, it will appear.

Working with a career professional can make it easier and speed up the process. Sometimes, connecting the dots and seeing the themes within your career takes a professional and objective view. This book intends to walk you through the process on your own (or in a group setting), but sometimes that's not enough. Give it a try first and seek further help if needed.

Here's what you need to know or find out to move forward: What are your most important values, where do your strongest interests lie, what type of personality do you have, what are you exceptionally great at doing, and what are your strongest skills? Let's discuss these topics one by one in the following chapters.

SUMMARY

- Work to understand yourself in order to progress in your career.

- Apply the AS.T.E.R. Career Model, as I did, to push yourself forward.

- Make the effort to gather feedback from people whose views you value.

- Go through this exciting process as you read through this book.

"I have learned that as long as I hold fast to my beliefs and values—and follow my own moral compass—then the only expectations I need to live up to are my own."

MICHELLE OBAMA

CHAPTER TWO

Values Are The Foundation

Values are very personal, and the combination of your strongest values will define you. They are the guiding principles that affect your daily actions, which in turn affect your entire life. Whether you realize it or not, your values guide your decisions. Your life, and, in turn, your career can be more harmonious if you take time to understand your values and honor them.

It can be helpful to take an inventory of your values periodically during your lifetime. Though most values remain a constant in your life, sometimes they evolve and change over time. For example, early in your career, money, and status may be more important to you. However, once you start a family, money and career can remain strong (in order to provide the best life for your family), or the importance of spending time with your family (rather than just providing for them) might supersede that value. Also, dramatic life changes can affect your value system. Often these involve some kind of loss—a loved one, dissolution of a marriage, foreclosure on a home, being fired unexpectedly, and so on.

Values can create internal conflict or provide internal harmony depending on how true you are to your own principles. In terms of variance, if security and stability are strong values for you, you may stay longer in a safe, well-paying job that doesn't really suit you. If family is a strong value, you may work in a job you don't enjoy just to put food on the table. Or, if you value your family highly, but you work in a job that requires many hours each week and lots of travel away from home, you will likely have conflicted feelings about your work because it's not compatible with your core value of spending time with your family.

On the other hand, work and personal values can align quite nicely. If your work matches your values well, you will feel less internal conflict and be more satisfied at home and at work. Think of a multinational professional who values world peace and works at the United Nations or a nurse who values health and spends days giving inoculations to patients. Can you see how aligning your values with your work could be very empowering?

Some people question the purpose of examining values when it comes to career planning. For a career advising professional, the effect values have on a career can seem very obvious, but most people don't see the connection. There is a strong association between your career and your values, and when they conflict, it usually leads to anxiety and discomfort. To make my point, I'll share a couple of examples. If you cherish the earth and consider yourself an environmental champion, you probably don't want to work for a company that exploits natural resources unsustainably. Or, if you are against war and military build-up of weapons, you may not want to work for a defense contractor.

Both of these examples illustrate a situation where personal values do not match the mission of an organization. This may seem trivial, and you might think, "I'm only an accountant at the company; it's not like I'm making the weapons." However, it is very likely that over time, the conflict of values will eat away at you consciously or subconsciously until you decide that the job is no longer working for you. You may not know exactly why, and you may blame it on a bad boss or other circumstances. You may even think that accounting is no longer your passion. While the other things may also be true, in most of these cases, it's mainly the conflict of values that is the issue. Finding a workplace or industry where your values align with your job will create a more satisfying career situation.

It's important to reflect on your values, which can be a very clarifying exercise. Review the list of values below and circle each value you highly cherish. If you want a different list of values to consider, go to

PassItOn at https://www.values.com/teaching-values for more ideas.

LIST OF 100 LIFE VALUES

Achievement	Diligence	Independence	Relaxation
Adventure	Discipline	Integrity	Recognition
Authenticity	Diversity	Intelligence	Reliability
Balance	Efficiency	Intuition	Resourcefulness
Beauty	Elegance	Joy	Risk-taking
Belonging	Empathy	Justice	Respect
Boldness	Energy	Leadership	Quality
Calm	Equality	Learning	Safety
Career	Excitement	Love	Self-control
Caution	Family	Loyalty	Service
Challenge	Faithfulness	Mastery	Security
Change	Fitness	Mentoring	Solitude
Collaboration	Freedom	Making a difference	Spirituality
Community	Friendship	Making money	Stability
Compassion	Fun	Morality	Strength
Competence	Gratefulness	Obedience	Structure
Competition	Growth	Openness	Speed
Consistency	Happiness	Orderliness	Success
Contribution	Hard work	Originality	Tolerance
Control	Harmony	Patience	Tradition
Cooperation	Health	Persistence	Truthfulness
Creativity	Helping others	Pleasure	Trustworthiness
Curiosity	Honesty	Pragmatism	Unity
Dependability	Humility	Precision	Variety
Determination	Humor	Productivity	Vision

Are there any values not listed that are important to you? If so, list them here.

_____

_____

_____

_____

_____

_____

Take a moment to reflect and write down your top life values in the space provided below. Just get them down on paper for now, and don't worry about any order.

_____

_____

_____

_____

_____

_____

The next step is to prioritize them. Select your top choices from those you circled or any you wrote in the sections above. Narrow them down to your top seven and then rank order those from most to least important.

My most important life value: _____

My next most important life value: _____

My next most important life value: _____

My next most important life value: _____

My next most important life value: _____

My next most important life value: _____

My next most important life value: _____

In addition to our life values, we also hold work values. They represent what we hold dear in the workplace. Let me share some statements that reveal what someone values about their work.

"I want to work for an employer who respects its employees." (dignity and transparency)

"I enjoy a fast-paced job." (speed and efficiency)

"I want to make a very high income." (money and security)

"Making a difference through my work is important to me." (personal impact)

"I want a job that challenges me to constantly grow." (learning)

Since this book is focused on your career, it's worth taking time to also assess your work values. Go to Brand Career Management at https://www.brandcareermanagement.com and complete the *Uncovering Your Work Values* worksheet. You can find a link to it on the homepage or the Resources page. Once done, rank order your top work values in the space provided below.

My most important work value: _____

My next most important work value: _____

My next most important work value: _____

My next most important work value: _____

My next most important work value: _____

My next most important work value: _____

My next most important work value: _____

I fully acknowledge that it can be hard to find a job or career that matches every one of your top values. That's why you need to prioritize them. Since most jobs will not incorporate all of them, knowing which ones are non-negotiable will help steer you toward jobs, careers, and organizations that hold those same values.

Because values play a critical role in career satisfaction, it is important to do some research on the values of your target companies and potential industries. Sometimes, you will find contradictory information. Though many companies state their mission and values in their marketing materials and on their websites, sometimes those values are not well represented in the day-to-day operations of the business. Talking to others who work at the company or with the company is often the best way to understand the true guiding principles of the organization. It's also a great way to network your way into an organization or industry. Even speaking to former employees of a company can be useful, and they are usually more willing to share a candid perspective.

It can be useful to look at your life and work values lists at the same time and see where there is overlap. If you value learning as a life value and growing on the job as a work value, this is a strong indication that learning in general is very important to you. This might steer you toward organizations that offer learning opportunities, such as schools, colleges, libraries, or online education. Notice where your life and work values converge and use this alignment as a compass to direct you to places where that belief is highly valued.

List five companies or organizations you can think of that emulate your top values.

Companies that share my values:

1) _____

2) _____

3) _____

4) _____

5) _____

If these places are not near your geographic location, try to list five more that are a commutable distance for you.

Local companies that share my values:

1) _____

2) _____

3) _____

4) _____

5) _____

In our post-COVID-19 world, more companies are interested in hiring remote workers. Go back to your top five list and research those companies' openness to remote working options.

Save this information in a safe place for future reference. Now that you have a better idea of the life and work values you hold right now, in the next chapter, we'll take a look at your interests.

Lauren's story

Let me share a client story that shows how clarifying your values can help you with your career pathing. When Lauren came to see me, she was at a career crossroads. After working for local non-profits in the disability community, she was self-employed for about 10 years. Her past roles were focused mainly on helping people with autism. She closed down her business and earned an MBA, but she wasn't sure what to do next. Even though she valued helping people, she had become burned out being an entrepreneur and being in a direct helping profession. She took time to reflect on what was really important to her and reaffirmed that she wanted a job that helped others but without being in the front line, preferably advocating for people with disabilities. She was considering fundraising and development, something with a non-profit, or anything helping others, but she was having trouble narrowing her focus to job titles.

She completed my Work Values Inventory and found her top values were to work in a structured environment within an institution that is respected and has integrity. She also wanted to work with the public for a fair wage while having fun. This led her to researching all of the non-profits in her area. She researched each of them to see how well they lived their mission. This included networking to learn more about the work environments and to uncover potential opportunities. Because of her values-driven job search, she found her way to a well-respected national non-profit with a regional office managing innovative services to people with disabilities. Once she found the right place based on a match in values, she was able to show where her skills would best fit, and they created a new role for her. This story shows how values can be a powerful factor in finding your next gig.

SUMMARY

- Values are a very important aspect of our lives and our career management.

- You need to assess and prioritize your strongest life values and work values.

- Once you know your most important work values, you can use this information to find places and work environments that match your values.

- Values are the first item in discovering your V.I.N.E.S. to help you find the best next directions for your career.

ACTIVITIES

For individuals

Did you complete the exercises in this chapter? If you did, who can you share them with?

For groups

If you are in a group, assign this chapter and the exercises for homework and review answers in a future meeting. One by one or in pairs, share the values you confirmed during the exercises. How did it feel to share your values with someone else? Did it make you feel more or less strongly about them?

"Career choice and progression doesn't have to fit into the standard societal mold. Do what you love and want to do. Find what you're good at, what you can sell or provide that is unique to you and go for it."

DANA DONOFREE, FOUNDER OF ANAONO

CHAPTER THREE

Interests Offer Insight

Interests are an important factor in assessing job fit and work environment compatibility. What fascinates us, keeps us engaged and motivated. Your hobbies and pastimes give clues about your preferences. It might not always have a strong or viable tie as a way to produce an income, but it is a reliable source of enjoyment for you. Knowing what we like gives us indicators of possible matches if we think broadly. For example, if you love volleyball and selling, you may not become a professional athlete, but you may be a good match for a marketing position for a company that produces sporting equipment. Sometimes, it's best for a hobby to remain a hobby, but sometimes it's worth looking into the viability of merging your interests with your career path. Knowing your interests can help you decide if certain jobs, careers, or work environments are compatible for you.

You may have revisited your interests in recent years, or maybe you haven't reconnected with them in a long time. Whichever is the case, it will benefit you to take some time to reflect and record them as you move your career forward. If it's been a while, you should note if your interests have changed. If you have assessed your interests in recent years, this exercise may only confirm what you already know, but making time for this simple confirmation is not a waste of time. Having insight into your top interests can help you see if there is any (obvious or unseen) alignment with your career path.

As you do this, think about some of these questions: What types of movies do you love to watch? What types of books do you read? What subjects do you always want to learn more about? Your answers give clues to your interests.

To get started, let's fill out some answers to the questions below.

Your favorite materials or media for relaxation are the following:

_____

_____

_____

_____

Your favorite materials or media for learning are the following:

_____

_____

_____

_____

Some of your all-time favorite books are the following:

_____

_____

_____

_____

What are you listening to (podcasts, TED Talks, etc.)?

_____

_____

_____

What are some of your favorite movies?

_____

_____

_____

_____

What are some of your favorite TV shows (now and in the past)?

_____

_____

_____

_____

What other content are you watching (YouTube, videos, etc.)?

_____

_____

_____

_____

What social media sites are your favorites?

_____

_____

_____

What is the purpose of the site (connection, information, photography)?

_____

_____

_____

_____

What do they focus on?

_____

_____

_____

_____

Name a childhood hero of yours.

_____

_____

_____

_____

What do you admire about this figure?

_____

_____

_____

What are some of your past hobbies?

_____

_____

_____

_____

What are some of your current hobbies?

_____

_____

_____

_____

What are some hobbies you'd like to learn more about?

_____

_____

_____

_____

What themes do you see among your answers so far? Do you notice any repeating subjects of interest? For example, do your interests lean toward fantasy or focus on the future? Do they center around science, people, ideas, or information? Do they evoke thoughts of mystery, happiness, humor, or human nature? Record any themes that seem to be coming to the surface.

Sometimes, the way we spend our free time reveals our interests. Because we spend so many hours at work, analyzing your current or most recent jobs for interests can be a useful exercise. Think about the subject(s) your job covers (athletics, business topics, helping others, solving problems). Take a moment to record your answers below. They could relate to the work itself and/or the company mission.

The types of subjects covered in my current job are the following:

The types of topics covered in past jobs that I enjoyed are the following:

_____

_____

_____

_____

If you volunteer, think about the places where you volunteer. Think about these questions: What is the mission of the organization? What role do you play as a volunteer? What do you enjoy about your volunteer experiences? How do they fulfill you?

Do you volunteer your time? If so, what types of roles do you fill and what are the types of organizations you help?

_____

_____

_____

_____

How does your volunteer work tie to your life and career interests?

_____

_____

_____

_____

_____

Do you see any themes emerging from the compilation of your interests? If so, record them here.

Theme #1: _____

Theme #2: _____

Theme #3: _____

Other themes:

_____

_____

_____

_____

Sometimes, it's hard to see the themes for yourself. If that's the case for you, try talking to others who know you well, and ask what themes they see based on your past experiences. Or you could hire a career professional to assist you. Helping identify the themes in people's lives is a frequent activity for career coaches and counselors. Nearly everyone could use assistance, even those trained in seeing the themes, so don't be too tough on yourself if you need support in this area. Another type of support, and a way to gather more information about your career, interests, and themes, could be to ask fellow members of a book club, job club, or other close group for input and feedback.

IT CAN BE HARD TO SEE YOUR OWN THEME

Sometimes, you are just too close to the situation to see the theme(s). For example, one of my clients, we'll call her Jane, came to me for help with her resume. Her educational background included biology and public health, and she was working on a nursing degree. She had held full-time jobs in health science, education, and recreation, and she had also worked part-time as a lifeguard and swimming coach.

Jane felt "all over the place" and unsure where to take her career moving forward. She felt she had worked in many jobs that didn't connect with each other. She couldn't see any theme and was having trouble marketing herself for a job search.

Go back to the first paragraph. Can you see her theme?

The theme was very obvious to me as it might be to you too: healthcare, specifically a passion for helping others stay healthy, fit, and safe. When I shared what I was seeing, she immediately agreed with me and thanked me for helping her see it too. Once stated, it was very obvious to her, but she admitted that, without help, she was not able to see the theme on her own.

Now, let's take this process a step further and delve deeper into your interests. In career counseling and coaching, we often use assessments to discover preferences. Questions, like the ones above, are considered informal assessment tools. Another way to uncover your interests is to discover your Holland Code, which you can obtain formally or informally. We'll try an informal way later in this chapter. At the end of this chapter, I'll share some resources that offer a more scientific way to uncover this information. You can try more than one way to discover your Holland Code and compare the results to see where they align.

Let's take a step back for a moment and explain who John Holland is and why his work matters to you. John Holland devoted his life to studying how interests and personality affect the work people do. His research suggests that people who perform jobs that match their code are more satisfied, stay longer, and contribute more to those jobs.

He sought out methods to match people to jobs that could be a good fit. In doing so, he created an assessment to measure people's interests. That's why it is called a Holland Code. This model can be extremely helpful in sorting out work, career, and job preferences to help you make informed choices. Not only can you use the code to describe people, but it's also useful when distinguishing between jobs and work environments.

Countless times his work has been borrowed and imitated. I think it's safe to say that it has been the most widely applied theory in the field of careers. You see the influence of it in many forms of career guidance and assessments. You can always tell a Holland Code because it uses some combination of six letters: R, I, A, S, E, and C. When taking a formal assessment, you receive a "score" for each letter.

Each letter describes types of people and how they relate to work. I'll describe each of the six letters below, using a compilation of many sources, including *What Color is Your Parachute?* by Richard Bolles, U.S. Department of Labor career websites, John Holland's work, my past work experience, and knowledge gained from past mentors and teachers.

These composites are generalizations. Not every person will fit neatly into only three categories, and not every word of each description will ring true for you. We each have a little bit of every letter within us, but some letters have a stronger pull for us than others. As you read each description, think about which resonates the most with you right now, and mark those that match well with your characteristics.

Realistic (R)

People who score high on "R" are generally interested in athletics, good with their hands, and prefer working with objects, machines, plants, or animals rather than people. They prefer doing the job without a lot of talk or argument (do it right the first time and get to the point). Realistic types often like to work outdoors and be active. It's torturous for an "R" to sit at a desk for eight hours a day. They tend to be stable, frank, practical, and self-reliant.

Investigative (I)

People who score high on "I" generally like to observe, learn, evaluate, or solve problems working with ideas and data. This type is often associated with scientific and academic pursuits. They like to analyze a problem, evaluate options and data, analyze results, and set a plan of action. They often prefer to work alone and tend to be analytical, independent, curious, and precise.

Artistic (A)

People who score high on "A" are driven by artistic expression. They like to work in unstructured situations using imagination and creativity. They prefer an innovative approach to problem solving and planning that relies heavily on intuition and imagination. For Artistic types, it is essential to put their creative spin on things. They are generally nonconforming, emotional, creative, idealistic, and not the most organized.

Social (S)

People who score high on "S" generally prefer to work with people in some helping capacity—informing, teaching, developing, coaching, or curing people. They prefer gathering data from all involved parties before generating an action plan. They will try to find solutions equitable for all concerned and are adept at networking with people and using words.

Social types like to work with people more than data, ideas, or objects. Some common traits for an "S" are understanding, helpful, tactful, sociable, and ethical. While many Social types are extroverted, it is possible to be an introverted person who is attracted to jobs that help people. If this is the case for you, it will be important to build in alone time and set firm boundaries for space to re-energize.

Enterprising (E)

People who score high on "E" generally like to work with people in a leadership capacity—managing, performing, persuading, and influencing, often for organizational, political, or economic gain. They prefer investigating a direct plan of action (to be carried out by others). They focus on achieving the goal and are not concerned with minor details. Enterprising individuals like to keep the big picture in mind.

Enterprising types often like to persuade and influence others to action. Most people in sales have an "E" in their Holland Code. A sales team manager would be the quintessential example of an "E" role. These types are often attracted to entrepreneurship and franchise opportunities. Enterprising types often take on leadership roles at work (managing a team) and in the community (PTA or HOA president). They are generally persuasive, energetic, and ambitious.

Conventional (C)

People who score high on "C" generally like to work with data and numbers more than with people or ideas. They also like to work with tangible things and have little tolerance for ambiguity. They like following instruction from others, rather than being in charge, and prefer following a defined and structured plan of action. They are attentive to detail and enjoy putting all the pieces of a plan together.

Conventional types often like to be systematic, organized, efficient, and orderly. They generally are rule followers who implement practical solutions. They are also accurate, conscientious, and self-controlled.

Think about yourself and reflect for a moment. What are the top three letters that describe you right now?

1) _____

2) _____

3) _____

4) _____

(It's okay to add a fourth if you're having trouble narrowing it down to three)

Now, let's talk a little more about these letters and how they can help you. Certain types of jobs, careers, and educational pursuits are tied to a combination of these letters. Some assessments and websites provide lists of job titles tied to Holland Codes (I'll revisit this later in the chapter). Below, I share a very limited list to get your mind flowing. Because some of the category titles could be ambiguous, I've added a few other words to each title using the common acronym of AKA (also known as).

Realistic (AKA Adventuring, Producing, or the Doers)

Some jobs that are a good match for Realistic types are auto mechanic (RIC), surgeon (IRA), truck driver (RCS), HVAC mechanic (RES), chef/cook (RSC) landscaper (RIS) and veterinarian (IRS).

Some fields of study that usually interest Realistic types include: engineering, criminal justice, architecture, and forestry.

Investigative (AKA Analytical)

Some jobs that are a good match for Investigative types include biologist (IAR), scientific and engineering programmer (IRE), psychiatrist (ISA), and airplane pilot (IRE).

Some fields of study that usually interest Investigative types include: engineering, biology, chemistry, physics, earth sciences, psychology, and law.

Artistic (AKA Creative)

Some jobs that are a good match for Artistic types often do not provide a stable income. Making it big and finding fame can be challenging for actors (AES), sculptors (AER), and instrumental musicians (ASC). Other roles where "A" types are more likely to provide reliable earnings include tattoo artist (AEC), interior designer (AES), copywriter (ASI), and web developer (ACI).

Generally speaking, any field of study that involves creative arts will interest Artistic types (such as theater, art, and music), along with graphic and design technology, art history, instructional media, and advertising/commercial art.

Social (AKA Helping People)

Some jobs that are a good match for Social types are career counselor (SAE), social worker (SEC), professional athletic coach (SRE), and homemaker (SEC).

Some fields of study that usually interest Social types include: communications, psychology, sociology, anthropology, history, education, and health.

Enterprising (AKA Influencing)

Some jobs that are a good match for Enterprising types are lobbyist (ESA) communications equipment supervisor (ERC), theater manager (ESR), financial planner (ESC), and fire marshall (ESR).

Some fields of study that usually interest Enterprising types include: business, finance, technology, and various majors related to management/administration/leadership.

Conventional (AKA Organizing)

Some jobs that are a good match for Conventional types are accountant (all accountant jobs except for tax accountant start with a "C"), court reporter (CSE), clinical data manager (CIS), budget analyst (CER), and accounting/budget clerk (CSR).

Some fields of study that usually interest Conventional types include: finance/accounting, administration/management, computer information systems, and library science.

Now, reflect once again and decide the top three that best describe you right now. Record these letters below.

_____   _____   _____

To gather this information in a more formal way, you can take validated assessments. One free resource is the O*NET Interest Profiler found on the My Next Move website at www.MyNextMove.org. This website is provided by the U.S. Department of Labor. After completing this assessment, you will see a number tied to each letter. Interpreting these results will reveal your Holland Code. Another free resource by the is Department of Labor O*NET, found at www.onetonline.org. This website allows you to view job descriptions that include a Holland Code (though they label it "Interests"). On this site, you can browse and search occupations using Holland Code terminology. If you are a college graduate, ask the career center of your institution if they provide any assessment tools to uncover your Holland Code. Also, ask if there is a charge or if it's free to alumni.

Another way to gather this information is to take paid assessments on your own or work with a career counselor. Be sure to ask if assessment fees are included in the total cost. Two commonly used assessments are the Strong Interest Inventory (SII) by CPP, Inc. and the Self-Directed Search (SDS) by PAR, Inc. Both of these paid assessments provide a list of compatible jobs tied to various Holland Codes. The SII should be administered by a qualified professional. The SDS is designed as a self-help tool, but most people get much more out of it if they discuss the results with a career professional.

Before ending this chapter, I'd like to share some nuances about the Holland Code that may be helpful to you.

Tips for working with your code

When taking a formal Holland Code assessment that produces a number for each letter, understand there are no "bad" scores. It is an assessment and not a test, so there are no wrong answers.

Even if you take a formal and scientifically validated assessment, you may not agree with the results. That is why career counselors will work with you to help interpret and confirm the results with you. Ultimately, whatever code you decide fits you best should be used as your Holland Code.

Jobs that can be a good fit do not have to match your Holland Code exactly. You always want to search for jobs that are coded with any combination of your top three letters. For example, I am an S-E-C, so I would explore jobs that are listed as SEC, SCE, ESC, ECS, CSE, and CES.

If you have one letter that is much higher than the rest, it can be useful to look through all jobs coded to start with that letter. If you have two letters that are the same score, you can look at a wider range of job titles to match both variations of your code.

You can use the Holland Codes in a variety of ways. The most common areas of application include jobs, careers, and work environments, but you can also use these insights when making decisions about volunteering and retirement activities, and educational and training opportunities, along with deciding which professional groups would be a good fit for you.

If all of the scores on each letter are low (for example, less than 10), you may need more involved assistance. Low scores across all letters might indicate someone who has had limited exposure to the world of work. Lower scores could also suggest motivational issues or that you need to work on some other things before your career (maybe you are going through a divorce, grieving for the loss of a loved one, or having some mental health issues).

If all of the scores on each letter are high (for example more than 40), you may have many strong interests. In this case, you may need additional help sorting out which areas you want to focus on now and what you might explore later in your career.

If you have equally high scores on "A" and "C," this suggests you are simultaneously creative and organized. This is a very rare combination, as these two letters are the most opposite of all six letters. Generally speaking, creative people are not extremely organized and organized people are not passionately creative. If you have this unique combination, view it as a strength rather than a weakness, and know that you may need to satisfy these two divergent interests in different ways.

- Where appropriate, market yourself as equally adept in both areas.

- You may seek a "C" type job and fulfill your "A" interests through hobbies or vice versa.

- You can look for "C" type jobs in an "A" type work environment (an accountant for an art gallery) or an "A" type job in a "C" environment (a web designer for an accounting firm).

Can you successfully do a job that does not exactly match your code? It's possible, but you may not enjoy it, and you are more likely to get bored or burn out quickly. I would avoid seeking out a job that is the exact opposite of your Holland Code. This would mean that your Holland Code is made up of three of the six letters (e.g., SCE), and the code of the job title you seek is made up of the remaining three letters (e.g., IRA).

If one of your dream jobs is not a good fit with your Holland Code, consider why. It could be that only one aspect of the job conflicts with your preferences and it's a small part of the role. Do more research to see how much of the job involves activities you don't enjoy. A job that does not fit your code may be able to satisfy you, but you need to go into it with open eyes knowing the parts of the job that may challenge you the most.

Limitations of the Holland Code

It's best to remember that interests are one area of self-knowledge. To get a fuller picture, you will want to combine this data with information on your values, skills, strengths, and personality as the Holland Code is only one piece of the puzzle. To get the most from it, combine it with insights gathered using other tools.

John Holland's research does not promise that if you do a job that matches your code, you will be perfectly happy in that job. Other factors get in the way (e.g., a bad boss, a toxic work environment, or a difficult geographic location). It's best to use the Holland Code as a guidepost, not as a silver bullet.

In that same vein, don't take the suggested job titles too literally. Sometimes, people get soured because they disagree with some of the job titles or very few jobs match their code. They get stuck on that, and they don't look at them in a broader sense. For example, you may not agree with the specific suggestion of "dentist," but try to look at the broader sense of that job as someone who likes to help others stay healthy, enjoys using her hands, and likes to work independently. Taking a broader view may help you come up with a title that is a good match but may not appear on the list.

When looking through a list of jobs tied to Holland Codes, know that it will have limitations because most lists are provided by (or based on those provided by) the Department of Labor. The government shares predicted job data, but it's not the best source for emerging job titles. Also, the information won't be the most up-to-date source for new jobs related to technology. For that information, you'll need to ask others who work in that field. O*NET does not list jobs held by only one person or very few people, such as President of the United States. It focuses on the majority of jobs that most people perform in the workplace. The list includes easily defined job titles such as daycare worker or sales manager, but it does not include more ambiguous titles like business owner, entrepreneur, or personal assistant. The list also does not include unique jobs like dolphin trainer, wedding planner, or an on-site tutor for child actors.

Know that the Holland Code framework doesn't work for everyone. I have found it works best for some types more than others. The concept is linear and less appealing to creative people who like to generate their own list of possibilities rather than use a pre-developed list. This framework is also more useful when there are many job titles from which to choose. Certainly, some codes (such as S-C-E) have more jobs tied to them than others. There are notably fewer job titles that include A and C because it's hard to find jobs that offer the opposing requirements of creativity and conformity. However, it is worth mentioning that some nursing jobs include both letters.

The Holland Code serves to help you make informed choices, but ultimately, it is not a panacea. It may reinforce what you already know about yourself (which will give you more confidence when pursuing jobs that match your code). It may remind you of past jobs that you enjoyed but have not thought about recently.

A final word on Holland Codes

It's important to realize that your interests can change over time. We are in a continuous cycle of finding new interests, dropping old interests, and retaining others for a lifetime. Knowing your strongest interests can help you find jobs and career paths that are likely to fulfill your current career aspirations.

You may not be able to make a living just following your passions and interests. You will need to do more research to see if pursuing a passion will bring in sufficient income. If realizing your passion requires you to start your own business, you may need to do more introspection. Not everyone is meant to be an entrepreneur. Realize that if you truly love making dessert pies (baker is R-S-E) and your research shows a viable market for opening a local pie shop, operating the bakery will require different skills (and different hours) than making the pies.

Moving forward, you will need to do research to see the job titles that are worth more investigation and narrow down your targets to a reasonable number. I would suggest shooting for two to four possibilities.

You can easily eliminate some things because the expected income doesn't meet your needs, there is little demand for that job in your geographic location, or you are not interested or able to take on new training that is required.

Now that you have completed exercises to uncover your values and interests, let's look into your personality.

Andrea's story

Andrea came to me at a time when she was exploring re-entry into the workforce after a long gap. She had worked in advertising early in her career but then put professionally paid work on hold while raising three children. Throughout her caregiving time, she was not only raising her kids but also helping significantly with both of her parents' elder care needs.

We were working on clarifying her interests, and she validated her Holland Code as S (27), E (20), and A (15). This made sense as she was always great with helping people, she has led many community organizing efforts, and she has always had a creative streak. This code, along with knowing her values and some brainstorming, produced potential new career paths to explore, including teaching art, promoting a sustainable environment, community outreach, advocacy, and opening an ice cream shop. Since she still had one child in high school, she needed a job that had part-time hours and was not too far from her home.

Ultimately, she ended up finding a job right in her backyard, so to speak. One day, she was looking at an information board at the nursing home where her mom lives. They were seeking someone for a part-time, temporary position to assist with resident activities. This seemed a perfect fit, so she inquired with the staff.

They were excited to have her apply. The staff had seen Andrea interact with her mom and knew she had the right demeanor to work with all of the residents. Andrea could see how the job fit into her Holland Code characteristics, and this gave her confidence to give it a try.

So far, it's working out beautifully, and one silver lining is that Andrea is able to see more of her mom. Due to COVID-19 restrictions, she had not been allowed to see her for a long time. Now, as a staff member, she can see her on a limited basis. The journey will not end here because the position was meant to be temporary. However, it was a great first step back into a paying position, and it's possible the need for the position will linger depending on the aftereffects of COVID-19.

As an update since I started writing this book, Andrea ended up leaving this job. As it turned out, post-COVID-19 they needed it to become a full-time position. Andrea was not ready to make that type of employment commitment with one child still in high school, so she turned down the opportunity. Still, she says that it was a great learning experience. It increased her confidence in her skills and in her ability to rejoin the workforce.

SUMMARY

- Focus on your interests because they help you assess job fit and work environment compatibility.

- Notice how you spend your time in and outside of work for additional clues to your interests.

- Assess your interests, and look for themes among your interests.

- Discover your Holland Code. The My Next Move website at www.MyNextMove.org, provides the O*NET Interest Profiler to assess your Holland Code for free.

- Remember that your Holland Code is a three-letter combination of the six letters that could make up a Holland Code (RIASEC).

- Use this information to find potential job titles to investigate further. Not all passions lead to a livable wage.

- Use the Holland Code wisely. It is a linear process and doesn't work for everyone, though I have seen it help many people.

ACTIVITIES

For groups

In addition to the exercises in the chapter, try some of these activities with a group.

Assign Chapter Three to the group (reading and the exercises). At the next meeting, briefly review the characteristics of each letter of the Holland Code. Then, try the activities below. Have people share their answers with the group one at a time. As an alternate method, pair attendees up and have each person discuss answers with each other. Allow enough time so that each person has a chance to speak.

1) Have each person share a summary of their answers to the questions and ask the listener(s) if they see a theme.

2) Share your Holland Code and why it resonates with you. Ask others to suggest jobs and careers that match the characteristics of your code.

"But in the long run, staying true to your temperament is key to finding work you love and work that matters."

SUSAN CAIN, AUTHOR OF *QUIET*

CHAPTER FOUR

Understand Your Natural Disposition

The "N" in V.I.N.E.S. stands for natural disposition, another area of self-assessment you will want to pursue because your personality can be a major factor in successful career management and your job search. Knowing your temperament can help you select jobs, careers, and work environments that will be a good fit. For example, someone who has a highly extroverted personality would likely need a job with a great deal of interaction with others for satisfaction and may be unfulfilled with work that requires long periods of time working in isolation. Though most jobs involve working with others, they can vary greatly on the amount of time working alone or in teams.

Many of our preferences in life relate to our personality type, and careers are no exception. It's important to know if you prefer spontaneity over planful and methodical actions. A more spontaneous and flexible person will likely be better at solving urgent and unexpected crises.

Do you make decisions using your head based on logical analysis, or are you more likely to decide based on how it will affect you and those around you? Are you most often drained of energy after being around other people for a long period of time? Or are you generally energized by being around people? These are important questions, and you will want to find out the answers to help you assess the best jobs and workplace environments for you.

Here are some questions to consider and complete.

In a few words, describe your personality; such as, I am an organized, planful, helpful, and friendly person.

_____

_____

_____

_____

Describe how your personality matches (or doesn't match) your current job, career path, or work environment.

_____

_____

_____

_____

What role do you think your personality is playing or not playing in your career satisfaction?

_____

_____

_____

_____

There are many personality assessments available; some are free, and some charge a fee. If you work with a career counselor or coach, ask if she is qualified to provide any personality assessments and if there are assessment fees. If you have taken personality assessments in the past, try to gather those results and review them to refresh your memory with that data. An assessment taken within the past few years would still be helpful, but if it's been a long time, you should reassess yourself.

The most well-known worldwide personality assessment is the Myers-Briggs Type Indicator assessment, and the book *Do What You Are* by Paul Tieger and Barbara Barron goes into extensive detail on how personality type affects job fit over your lifetime. That book gets quite technical, but it is an excellent resource if you would like to dig deeper into this area. For this book, I am covering more areas than just personality, so I will not go into nearly as much depth on this one aspect.

As a starting point, try to identify your personality preferences informally. For continuity, I am using the Myers-Briggs terminology, though their category headings can be misleading, so please don't get caught up with those words. Focus more on the statements underneath, rather than the headings.

**Please put a check mark next to the phrases
that are true for you most of the time.**

The statements in the two columns that follow are related to where you direct your energy and how you interact with the world.

EXTROVERTED

○ I feel energized from being around people.

○ I often focus my attention outward.

○ I often ask myself, "How will this affect others?"

○ I have a wide network.

○ I often think things through out loud.

○ I like talking to others.

○ I often speak before I think.

○ I talk more than listen.

○ I don't mind being the center of attention.

○ I generally prefer being around others.

INTROVERTED

○ I often think before I speak.

○ I enjoy solitude.

○ I keep a few close and trusted friends.

○ I find parties and social events draining.

○ I often ask myself, "How does this affect me?"

○ I listen more than talk.

○ I avoid being the center of attention.

○ I often focus my attention inward.

○ I need to think things through by myself.

○ I enjoy tasks that require focus and concentration.

The statements in the following two columns relate to how you gather information and whether you are more present-focused or future-focused.

SENSING

○ I focus on facts and details.

○ I don't naturally see the forest for the trees.

○ I am detail-oriented.

○ I focus on the here and now.

○ I am very practical.

○ I need specific information to operate well.

○ I don't mind repetition.

○ I prefer to work in a methodical order.

○ I gather information sequentially.

○ I follow directions.

INTUITIVE

○ I am open and adaptable.

○ I can see patterns easily.

○ I am constantly creating ideas.

○ I naturally see the big picture.

○ I focus on the future.

○ I always see the possibilities.

○ I enjoy using my imagination.

○ I like to theorize.

○ I don't always follow directions.

○ I listen to my hunches and can anticipate well.

The statements in the following two columns are tied to how you make decisions and relate to others.

THINKING

○ I enjoy using reason.

○ I pride myself on being rational.

○ I use objective criteria to make decisions.

○ I enjoy analyzing situations.

○ I usually see things clearly in black and white.

○ I can be unemotional and impersonal at times.

○ I use my head more than my heart to make decisions.

○ I am motivated by achievement.

○ I make fair and unbiased decisions.

○ I prefer logical order.

FEELING

○ I often seek harmony.

○ I think logic may be overrated.

○ I prefer to make decisions based on my heart and values.

○ I often consider others when making decisions.

○ I'm told by others that I am motivational and inspirational.

○ I value the warmth of relationships.

○ I enjoy being appreciated.

○ I want to understand others and myself.

○ I possess excellent interpersonal skills.

○ I am able to empathize with others.

The statements in the following two columns are related to how you present yourself to the world and how much structure you prefer.

JUDGING

○ I usually know what my weekend plans are by midweek.

○ I prefer an orderly environment.

○ I am goal-oriented.

○ I pride myself on being organized.

○ I prefer to work in a methodical order.

○ I plan ahead to avoid surprises.

○ I don't mind having rules to follow.

○ I make decisions easily.

○ I work first, play second.

○ I like predictability.

PERCEIVING

○ I am able to go with the flow.

○ I tend to keep my options open.

○ I enjoy spontaneity.

○ I am open-minded to change and possibilities.

○ I am a very curious person.

○ I prefer to remain flexible.

○ I welcome change and variety.

○ I am adaptable.

○ I prefer fewer rules.

○ I avoid routine and enjoy unpredictability.

Add up the checkmarks for each list and record the totals below. Note: If the number is a tie, look at the statements and pick the set that overall captures your preference the best.

EXTROVERTED (E) ○   **INTROVERTED (I)** ○

1) Circle the letter with more check marks, E or I.

SENSING (S) ○   **INTUITIVE (N)** ○

2) Circle the letter with more check marks, S or N.

THINKING (T) ○   **FEELING (F)** ○

3) Circle the letter with more check marks, T or F.

JUDGING (J) ○   **PERCEIVING (P)** ○

4) Circle the letter with more check marks, J or P.

Taking one letter from each line should give you a four-letter code, which can be tied to a Myers-Briggs type.

_____	_____	_____	_____
E or I	**S or N**	**T or F**	**J or P**

To confirm the above code, read the descriptions below to see if you continue to agree with the preference for one letter over another in each of the four dichotomies.

Energizing

Extroversion (E): People who strongly identify with this category are often interested in people and things and draw energy from activities and people in the outside world.

Introversion (I): People who strongly identify with this category are often interested in ideas in their mind and draw energy from their own emotions and impressions.

Perceiving

Sensing (S): People who strongly identify with this category are often interested in what is real and focus on what can be seen, heard, and touched in the present.

Intuitive (N): People who strongly identify with this category are often interested in what can be imagined and focus on what might be and the future.

Deciding

Thinking (T): People who strongly identify with this category are often interested in what is logical and focus on organizing and structuring information to make objective decisions.

Feeling (F): People who strongly identify with this category are often interested in what's important and focus on organizing and structuring information to make values-oriented decisions.

Living

Judging (J): People who strongly identify with this category are often interested in organizing and focus on living a planful life.

Perceiving (P): People who strongly identify with this category are often interested in adapting and trying things out and focus on living a spontaneous life.

There are 16 possible types using all possible combinations of the preferences: ISTJ, ISFJ, INFJ, INTJ, ISTP, ISFP, INFP, INTP, ESTP, ESFP, ENFP, ENTP, ESTJ, ESFJ, ENFJ, and ENTJ. Circle the type that most resembles you.

Your four-letter code can be a starting point in assessing your personality. It would be best to take a more formal assessment to validate your results because this activity is a very cursory way to determine your personality type. Websites offering free access to a Myers-Briggs type are shared at the end of this chapter. Also, the strength of your preference is important. Each of these dichotomies is on a continuum. Knowing the potency of each preference provides further clarity.

As an example, I am a very strong "J," and I exemplify the preferences of a "J" type person to an extreme. However, when it comes to "T" and "F," I am very close to the middle. My preferences for "J" and "F" could be diagrammed as below.

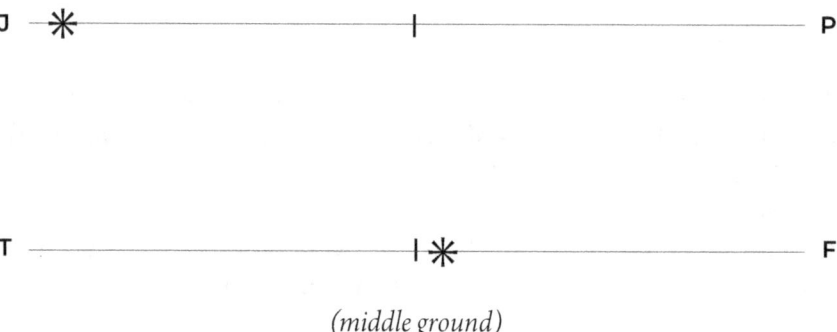

(middle ground)

Since my preference for "F" is close to the middle, it suggests it is a slight preference, and therefore my response to a decision-making situation could vary depending on the circumstances. In contrast, my preference for "J" (structure over spontaneity) is strong, and therefore my response to a situation will be more predictable. For example, I will almost always prefer to have order and rarely will I initiate change. To put this in career terms, jobs with too much change and variety would not suit me, but those with some stability, predictable tasks, and the ability to have control over my schedule would be a good fit. However, someone with a strong preference for P would do well in a less structured work environment where each day's tasks are unpredictable.

If you feel very split down the middle, have no fear. This means that you are more flexible about those traits. Consider it a selling point that you are adaptable rather than a flaw that your preference is not clearer.

For example, if your preference is only slightly leaning toward introversion or extroversion, you might be an ambivert. Ambiverts are people who can easily switch from the qualities of an extrovert or introvert depending on the situation. If you don't have a strong preference for sensing over intuitiveness, you can probably easily be in the present and get things done, but, when needed, you can be imaginative and futuristic. If you are in the middle of thinking and feeling, you're able to think logically and objectively when making decisions but can also recognize when a situation requires more empathy and possibly a bending of the rules. If you are straddling between judging and perceiving, you can be structured and orderly but also can change things up and be okay with unexpected change.

Focusing on a person's temperament in order to analyze their personality provides another useful lens for career changers. David Keirsey has done extensive research on this topic and has determined four temperaments from the 16 types. They are NF, NT, SP, and SJ. These temperaments can be derived from your type by finding the two letters in your four-letter type that match one of the temperaments. For example, my type is an ESFJ, and therefore my temperament is SJ. On the Keirsey website at https://keirsey.com/temperament-overview/, you can click on a temperament to learn more about each one. Below is a brief description of each temperament with percentages obtained from the Keirsey website.

NF: Keirsey calls NFs the Idealists and suggests they make up 15% of the population. This temperament seeks harmony and clarity of self-identity. NFs are often catalysts for change. They motivate others and empathize strongly with people. They need encouragement and are sensitive to conflict. One area for development would be feeling less driven by obligation and guilt as NFs often put the needs of others above their own and have difficulty saying no, so they sometimes take on too much. NF's are commonly found in jobs such as teachers, counselors, healers, and social workers.

NT: Keirsey calls NTs the Rationals and suggests that they make up 10% of the population. People with this temperament seek competency. NTs are often visionaries and operate in a logical way. They hold high expectations of themselves and others and abhor incompetence. NTs are typically intellectually curious and non-conforming, enjoy complexity, and are high achievers. Due to their logical and independent style, NTs might come across as aloof or arrogant. Typical jobs that are a good match for NTs would be lawyer, computer programmer, judge, architect, and analyst.

SJ: Keirsey calls SJs the Guardians and suggests they make up 45% of the population. This temperament seeks stability and belonging. SJs often bring order from chaos and hold membership in organizations that are dear to them. They are your "steady eddies." They have difficulty operating in disorganized environments and fare much better in structured work environments with clearly defined expectations. SJs should fare well in occupations related to logistics, administration, and finance or any job where order is key to success and deadlines are common. Routines will not bother or bore an SJ; in fact, they prefer them.

SP: Keirsey calls SPs the Artisans and suggests they make up 30% of the world's population. This temperament seeks action. It is very hard for an SP to sit at a desk all day long, especially doing repetitive or monotonous tasks. Routine is their nemesis. They thrive on troubleshooting and negotiating and are excellent problem solvers in a crisis. This is the type of person you want to take charge in a fire. So maybe it's no surprise that a firefighter is an SP type of role, along with airline pilot, air traffic controller, or any job that is highly action-oriented and relies on the person's ability to navigate unexpected circumstances.

Read each description above and see which temperament you identify with the most. It's possible you connect with more than one, and that is okay. We all have a little of each temperament within us, but usually one is dominant. Now go back to the previous exercise and see if there are repeats of the two letters from your dominant temperament within your four-letter code. For example, I have the temperament of an SJ, and my four-letter type is ESFJ, so they align well and validate each other. I definitely see some of the NF traits within me, but the SJ temperament is by far the strongest, and I don't identify with most of the characteristics of the SP or NT temperaments.

Final thoughts

It can be hard to come by a complete list of job titles that match each type or temperament, but there are many partial lists. You can find lists in this infographic at Novorésumé, which can be found at https://novoresume.com/career-blog/career-paths-for-every-personality and on PersonalityPage.com, at www.personalitypage.com. Click on the icon labeled Careers from the home page.

Two free online assessment tools can help determine your type. A great site to help determine a Myers-Briggs type is 16Personalities.com at https://www.16personalities.com/. Click on Take the Test to begin. This assessment is offered in 37 languages. You can see a description of all 16 Myers-Briggs types at PersonalityPerfect.com at this page: https://www.personalityperfect.com/16-personality-types/. Another site for assessing temperament is Keirsey.com at www.keirsey.com, which showcases the research of David Keirsey.

Remember that every personality type is valuable. There is no better type than another, and type does not determine intelligence, mental stability, or likelihood of success. It's important to look at personality as one facet of an entire human being and not pigeonhole others. Knowing your temperament can be valuable and give you great insight for your career direction. Take time to find out your personality type and use the information to find work that best suits you.

Cassie's story

Your personality type can have an impact on your career management in a few ways: your work environment, how you manage a job search, and ultimately your career path. Let me share Cassie's story as an example of these points.

Cassie is an attorney who identifies as an ESFJ. The SJ temperament keeps her focused and goal oriented, even when the chips are down. Her best skills are planning, organizing, interviewing for information, and negotiating. After having a successful and high-paying career in healthcare law and risk management, Cassie had a progression of unfortunate incidents. She went through a divorce, and shortly afterward, she was laid off for the first time and lost her sister. Next, she found employment in a series of short-term contractual assignments with questionable companies, which made her consider leaving healthcare altogether. During this time, she had a few health issues of her own, including multiple surgeries. Through it all, she persevered by leveraging her personality type.

We worked together over the course of a few years while she sought a full-time job with a reputable firm that allowed her to utilize her legal background and experience in managing healthcare risks. She was great about staying in touch with her connections, which proved highly valuable. In fact, almost every short-term assignment she landed was a result of networking. This was Cassie putting her preference for extroversion to good work. She used her organizational skills to keep track of who she had spoken with and when to follow up. Most importantly, she created structure to manage her long-term job search and pace herself while she simultaneously worked short-term gigs to pay the bills and care for three young adults as a single mom.

Her persistence paid off. Each temporary assignment exposed her to new people and organizations. One of her last short-term assignments required collaboration with a reputable and highly successful consulting firm. In one of the virtual meetings for a project she was on, she gave legal advice in her professional and matter-of-fact way. Unbeknownst to her, someone was listening in on the meeting and was impressed by her words and guidance. Later, she was invited to an interview with his firm. Eventually, she landed a job with this organization. This new role utilizes all of her organizational abilities to keep projects on time but now she has more financial stability and status, and the freedom to set her own hours and location. Those benefits align well with her work values and now she is proud to share the name of her employer.

SUMMARY

- Your personality is an integral part of who you are and has a significant effect on the types of job and work environments that will be a good match for you.

- Discover and validate your personality type and your temperament.

- Combine this information with your values and interests to gain a broader scope of reference for your career management.

- Apply this information to uncover jobs and career paths that would be a good fit.

ACTIVITIES

For groups

In addition to the exercises in the chapter, try some of these activities with a group.

Assign Chapter Four for your group (reading and the exercises). At the next meeting, try the activities below. Have people share their answers with the group one at a time. As an alternate method, pair attendees up and have each person discuss answers with each other. Allow enough time so that each person has a chance to speak.

1) Have each person share the letters of their personality type or temperament and the characteristics of that type that ring true for them.

2) Discuss the hallmarks of each type represented in the group. As a group, brainstorm jobs and careers that match each personality type.

"While we have the gift of life, it seems to me the only tragedy is to allow part of us to die— whether it is our spirit, our creativity or our glorious uniqueness."

GILDA RADNER

CHAPTER FIVE

Embrace Your Exceptional Qualities

Everyone has unique gifts and strengths. Another word for strength is superpower. Do you know what yours are? If you do, great. I hope you are using them on a regular basis. If you don't, you need to sort this out. Why? Because your life and career are easier when you leverage your strengths. Work may also be less stressful and more effortless. I'm not saying that you will not encounter challenges when applying your strengths, but it will certainly be easier to get things done using them, rather than fighting against your weaknesses.

When speaking about strengths and weaknesses, there are generally two perspectives. One promotes trying to overcome your weaknesses. The other suggests that you build upon and focus on your strengths, while also finding ways to compensate for your weakness, such as hiring someone to do that part of the work, delegating to others, etc. I believe in the latter approach. I'm not saying that we should never try to work on our weak areas, but I do believe that it's not worth your time and energy trying to mitigate a weakness. Your time is much better spent uncovering your strengths and finding ways to put them to use.

So, "What is your superpower?" Can you answer that question in a heartbeat? Don't feel badly if you can't right now because that's true of many people. Sometimes, we have been discouraged from naming and embracing our superpower, or we are unaware of it. Other times, we have an inkling about our greatest strengths, but we are hesitant to shed light on them. This chapter intends to help you flesh out your exceptional abilities.

I know you turn to certain people for their superpowers. In fact, I bet you can name one person quickly for each task below where you might need assistance:

- Looking your best for a high-level event
- Planning a big event with many attendees
- Figuring out a new technology tool
- Solving a scheduling issue
- Choosing décor for a room

You ask these folks for help because they are great at something. It just seems to come naturally to them, and they don't mind that you asked for help because they enjoy using their superpower.

Let's try to figure out your superpower(s). Record answers to the questions below and jot down any thoughts that come to mind.

What do people ask you for help with on a regular basis?

_____

_____

_____

When you think about feedback you have gotten over the years (from friends, bosses, colleagues, etc.) what comments, words, and qualities come up over and over again?

_____

_____

_____

_____

Which of your talents or personal strengths receive frequent praise?

_____

_____

_____

_____

No matter what you do for a living, what is the easiest part of the job for you?

_____

_____

_____

_____

In general, what things have always come easily to you?

_____

_____

_____

_____

What type of activities do you often volunteer to do (in any setting)?

_____

_____

Strengths are unique superpowers

Superpowers, while linked to skills, are different. We usually think of skills in a professional context, and many people doing the same job have similar skill sets. For example, most accountants are good with numbers. Many have similar accounting abilities gained from experience and/or education. But each accountant could have a different superpower. One might be great at explaining accounting principles to others who are not accountants (communicating superpower). One might be extremely organized and always has client taxes done ahead of time (efficiency superpower). Another could be great at connecting you to other needed resources (networking/connecting superpower). In the examples above, all of the women can apply accounting skills to keep finances legitimate and complete tax forms, but each of them has a unique superpower.

The uniqueness of your superpower is where the phrase "unique value proposition" comes from, but we don't need fancy titles for our strengths to make use of them. You mainly need to know what makes you unique through your superpowers. You may have more than one. Your strength might be unique because few people share it. Or it might be that you offer a unique combination of abilities, including your superpower. For example, being organized is my superpower. In general, being organized is not an unusual strength, and it's not a required skill for career professionals. However, as a career coach in private practice, being organized can be a superpower for me. It helps me keep my business in order, and this superpower helps me empower my clients to stay focused as they go through their career journey process.

Once you embrace your superpowers, you can identify jobs and career paths that require those talents, and this will put you closer to jobs that are satisfying and feel authentic. Knowing your unique strengths can also help you endorse yourself. Be sure to market your strengths when writing your resume and sharing about yourself (when networking and in interviews). You can highlight them in interview answers, and incorporate words of strength into your career summary on your resume. Use your strengths as a foundation for any personal branding efforts. For example, when building your profile on LinkedIn or setting up a virtual presence, be sure to include words that highlight your superpower. A sentence such as "I am a trustworthy, organized, and reliable career coach who can help you figure out your next career move faster" incorporates my strengths of being a dependable and efficient truth-teller. I could use this sentence in a number of places in my personal branding to highlight my strengths.

Sharing your superpower(s)

Once you have identified your greatest strengths, you will want to share them with the world in constructive ways. Personal branding pioneer and guru William Arruda has written two books to help you with this process. The influential book he co-authored, *Career Distinction,* explains how you can express your brand to make a lasting impression. His later book, *Digital You,* focuses on the digital side of personal branding. Both books are very helpful in building your brand.

I know it can be hard to talk about how good you are at certain things, but if you don't share your strengths, there may be no other way for others to know about them. There is a great book called *BRAG! The Art of Tooting Your Own Horn Without Blowing It* by Peggy Klaus. It walks you through the process of uncovering stories and strengths and how to share them without feeling uncomfortable. I highly recommend it.

Blindspots

A very common barrier to discovering our superpower is that we are blind to it. Since a superpower is an ability that comes easily, we are apt to discount it or think that everyone has this capacity. I can personally attest to this phenomenon as I was well into my forties before I fully embraced the fact that I am more organized than the average person. When I took time to really dwell on it, I realized, that during my whole life, I've been driven to put things in order, and people have been asking me to help them organize things. Even still, it took some reflection and honesty to understand, then claim, and now embrace my drive to organize. I'm sure you have superpowers that you have written off as something "everyone else can do too," but they probably can't do it nearly as well as you!

Formal ways to find your superpower(s)

If you need more help to uncover your exceptional abilities, try a more formal approach. You can take the CliftonStrengths assessment by Gallup (formerly Strengths Finder) by going to https://www.gallup.com/clifton-strengths. You can also buy the book to obtain the code that allows you to take the assessment online. The book itself is small with the bulk of the content in Part II, which explains the 34 traits being measured. After you complete the assessment, it will identify your top five talents. Use the book or the online information to read about your unique strengths and ways to develop them even further. In 2020, Marcus Buckingham created the StandOut online assessment, which serves a similar purpose. You can find it on Marcus Buckingham's site at https://www.marcusbuckingham.com. It pulls out your top two superpowers from a set of nine and explains how you can leverage those strengths. So far, it has been offered to the public for the cost of sharing your email and joining their email list.

Another great tool is available from 360 REACH found at https://www.reachcc.com/reach/survey.nsf/page/home. This useful online tool developed by William Arruda helps uncover your brand from a different perspective. The system collects data on how others view your strengths and personal brand. It is free, but there are upgrade options with additional fees. The process involves asking others to complete a short questionnaire. The free version requires you to collect information within 14 days, which begins the moment you sign up. Therefore, I suggest you consider who you want to ask and gather those emails before registering on the site. The report provided gives you a summary of the responses, and you can hire a professional to help you interpret the findings.

Deborah's story

Let me share how one of my clients learned to recognize her superpower. Deborah was a mid-career female client moving into a high-level corporate role. I was given background information before our first meeting. Consistent feedback showed that others saw Deborah as innovative, dedicated, and efficient. She was starting a new role in a company where she had worked for a few years. The organization had recently created this position to improve communication and processes for corporate initiatives across the organization. She was feeling overwhelmed and wasn't sure where to start. She was also feeling doubtful of her abilities. Yet, earlier in this conversation, she had stated that she was feeling similar to a prior time just before she had initiated a new company program that turned into a huge success. I pointed out that the skills she implemented in that situation were exactly the same skills needed in this new situation. I suggested that her superpowers could be one of the compelling reasons the company selected her for this new post. After some contemplation, she agreed with me that she did have these skills, and, in fact, they were a unique combination of talents needed for this challenge, but she hadn't seen that point of view until that moment. She was now ready for the challenge ahead with more confidence in her strengths.

SUMMARY

- Everyone has strengths. It's important to know yours.

- Take time to uncover your superpowers, embrace them, and learn to apply them to your work.

- This is the fourth piece of your V.I.N.E.S. Add it to the other information to find employment opportunities and situations that draw on your strengths.

ACTIVITIES

For groups

In addition to the exercises in this chapter, try some of these activities with a group.

1) Ask each person in the group to share the top strength of every other person in the room. Have someone document each answer. Give time for reflection and have group members think of an example from their life that proves the superpower. Ask for volunteers to share their story.

2) Have each group member share a summary of the answers from this chapter and name a superpower(s). Allow the group to react to each person's answer to see if they align with other group members' perceptions of the individual. If any misalignments are revealed, discuss possible explanations. In some cases, people could have more than one superpower or they might be blind to their own strengths.

"What I wanted was to be allowed to do the thing in the world that I did best–which I believed then and believe now is the greatest privilege there is. When I did that, success found me."

DEBBI FIELDS, THE CREATOR OF MRS. FIELDS

CHAPTER SIX

Skills Are The Final Piece

The final piece of the assessment puzzle is your skill set. Just as it's necessary to know your values, interests, natural abilities, and exceptional qualities, it is equally important to know what skills you enjoy using and feel qualified to implement.

Skills fall into three categories: technical, personal, and transferable. Sometimes the lines between the definitions of each of these groupings blur. Therefore, don't get hung up on which list to add a skill to. Rather, make your end focus to narrow down all of the skills you possess by how good you are at them and how much you enjoy using them. Most often we use our skills for paid employment, but skills can be present in all areas of our lives. Below, I share a brief definition of each type of skill and ask you to respond with words that are true for you in that area.

1) *Technical/job-specific skills.* These often are learned through education and/or on-the-job experience. They often involve specialized knowledge. Some of them can be utilized in more than one career, but usually they are most helpful to a specific job or field. Some examples include an architect creating blueprints, a graphic designer using Photoshop, or a counselor knowing therapeutic theories and techniques. Other examples could include work involving machinery, equipment, customized software, and proprietary systems.

List 10 job-specific skills you currently possess or have utilized in the past.

1) _____

2) _____

3) _____

4) _____

5) _____

6) _____

7) _____

8) _____

9) _____

10) _____

Of these technical skills, which do you still enjoy using?

_____

_____

_____

_____

2) *Personal traits.* These could be some of your strengths or personality characteristics (being on time, dependable, enthusiastic, thoughtful, having a positive attitude, etc.). Some positive traits are referred to as soft skills (friendly, easygoing, fair, etc.). They are about your character and can be applied to many jobs, though some jobs will be a better fit for some traits (for example, being a planful woman will help you succeed in roles that require thinking ahead and planning out events, but it may not be an

asset in roles that require spontaneity, handling unexpected crises, or jobs with lots of ambiguity). Knowing these skills can help you in choosing a suitable work environment, and some employers will hire specifically for these soft skills (especially when the job-specific skills can be taught and learned easily).

List 10 personal traits that describe you. (Hint: You can use answers from previous chapters.)

1) _____

2) _____

3) _____

4) _____

5) _____

6) _____

7) _____

8) _____

9) _____

10) _____

Which of these traits is strongest for you?

_____

_____

_____

_____

3) *Transferable skills.* These skills are action verbs that can be used in a variety of jobs. When you are trying to get unstuck or considering a career change, it's best to focus on your transferable skills because, as the name implies, these are the skills that are easiest to transfer to a new role, career, or field. Some common transferable skills are teaching, managing events, and supervising. Sometimes, they are soft skills, such as communicating, leading, and mentoring. In most cases, these skills will help you land your next employment opportunity, so you need to be adept in explaining yours.

If you want to take a full inventory of your transferable skills, go to Brand Career Management at brandcareermanagement.com. You can download the free Transferable Skills Inventory by scrolling down the home page or going to the Resources page. You can also pay for online assessments to gain clarity of your skill set through SkillScan at https://www.skillscan.com/ or the Motivated Skills Inventory by Richard Knowdell found at https://www.careerplanner.com/Knowdell-Motivated-Skills-CardSort.cfm.

If you don't have time to complete a full inventory, take a few minutes to write down your transferable skills below.

List 10 transferable skills you possess.

1) _____

2) _____

3) _____

4) _____

5) _____

6) _____

7) _____

8) _____

9) _____

10)_____

Since these skills are often the key to your next role, think about where your transferable skills would fit in the grid below. It's useful to think of your transferable skills falling into four categories. You could call them the A, B, Cs of skill satisfaction. Each quadrant on the grid below represents your relationship with a skill. The relationship changes depending on how much you enjoy using a skill and how good you are at it.

Q1) You don't enjoy them and are not good at them (AVOID).

Q2) You don't enjoy them, but you're good at them (BURNOUT).

Q3) You enjoy them, and you are good at them (BLISS).

Q4) You enjoy them but are not good at them (CHALLENGE).

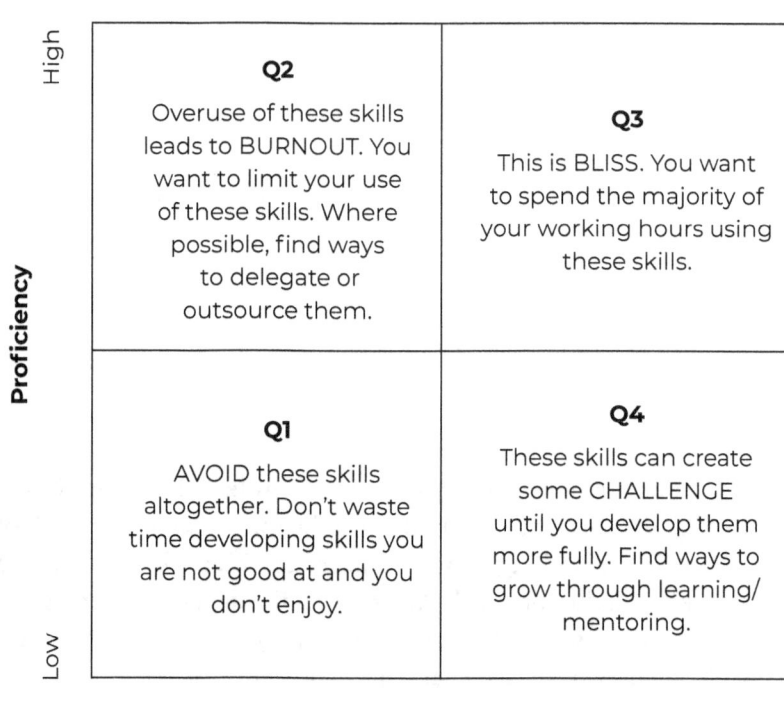

Proficiency — High / Low

Q2
Overuse of these skills leads to BURNOUT. You want to limit your use of these skills. Where possible, find ways to delegate or outsource them.

Q3
This is BLISS. You want to spend the majority of your working hours using these skills.

Q1
AVOID these skills altogether. Don't waste time developing skills you are not good at and you don't enjoy.

Q4
These skills can create some CHALLENGE until you develop them more fully. Find ways to grow through learning/ mentoring.

Level of enjoyment

Don't enjoy   Enjoy

Use the grid below to fill in your transferable skills in the quadrant that represents your feelings about the skill. Ideally, you would have five to 10 skills listed in Q3. From this list, you can brainstorm jobs that use these skills. There may be times when you don't want to take a skill forward with you, and that's okay. While you may remain good at something your entire career, your enjoyment in using that skill may fluctuate at times, depending on the work environment and/or your phase in life. For example, you might be a great supervisor, but you may choose to take roles that don't require managing others while you raise young children. Right now, decide what skills you want to focus on using in the coming years.

	Proficiency High	
Q2 Skills that are strengths that I DO NOT enjoy using:	**Q3** Skills that I enjoy using and do quite well:
Q1 Skills that DO NOT interest me, and I don't think I do well:	**Q4** Skills I would like to develop:

Proficiency

High

Low

Level of enjoyment

Don't enjoy   Enjoy

Elizabeth's story—the power of transferable skills

When I met Elizabeth, she had been working as a salesperson in a toxic environment at a healthcare company for about six years. The last few years had been very stressful, but she had been doing all that was asked and meeting sales goals. Then suddenly, they laid her off. This caused her to take a new look at her career path.

At first, she was adamant that she didn't want to do sales anymore. Since she expressed a desire for a new direction, we went through the full gamut of assessments for skills, interests, personality, and values. As she worked through the process, she realized that she really did love using the skills of selling and customer service. She also realized that selling was a good fit for her personality. She enjoyed working in teams where there was a friendly amount of competition. It became obvious that selling was still her passion, but a long-term bad work environment had almost tricked her into leaving that type of work. The solution was to find a new industry for her transferable skill set.

She researched a few paths and ultimately chose to become a real estate agent. This required learning new technical skills and taking a test to become licensed. She aligned with a seasoned realtor who recognized her talent at selling. This broker was also willing to teach someone new to real estate. Elizabeth has stayed with that company and established herself as a successful agent on a top selling team. It was slow going at first, but through her determination, she has found a new path that she really enjoys.

Expressing your skills

Now that you have better clarity on the skills you possess, you need to find ways to share them with potential clients and employers. Keep a list of your top skills handy and visible for continued focus on which skills you want to develop in your next role. This is helpful for comparing opportunities as they come your way. It's also a good idea to create something that is sharable with others.

Lauren's story continued

I mentioned Lauren in Chapter Two, where I shared how her values played a role in her job search. I'd like to point to her story again regarding skills. After Lauren went through the process of analyzing her transferable skills, she created a document that she consistently shared and brought to all meetings related to job search. The list was also helpful to Lauren because she used it as a checklist for what skills should be needed in her next job. Even though she was having trouble coming up with specific job titles to target, she knew the right fit would involve using these skills.

Lauren was diligent about networking and focused on leaders she admired running non-profits in her community. After a few months of job search, Lauren's networking efforts provided her with a meeting with a respected leader in the community. This leader had a reputation as a visionary, and she ran one of the top non-profits helping people with disabilities. In the meeting, Lauren shared her top skill list with the leader and kept in touch.

In the end, that leader created a position for Lauren that involved managing programs to help employ people with disabilities. Sharing this list with her future employer helped the CEO see where Lauren could add value to the organization. They started a discussion one day that ended up in a job offer, starting first as a consultant and then turning into a full-time job with benefits. Below, you can see the list of her top skills (with her permission). Her hard copy version was on an 8.5 x 11 piece of paper with a border of small yellow stars.

Lauren's skill strengths

1. Build relationships to match needs with resources and services.

2. Serve as a liaison between entities to discover gaps then determine solutions.

3. Manage projects to enhance quality of life for vulnerable populations.

4. Initiate new ideas based on assessments and/or rubric criteria to perform at higher level.

5 Interview clients or staff to uncover unspoken issues.

6. Utilize listening skills and organizational skills to optimize processes within organization or for consumer experience improvement.

7. Provide care and support to a diverse team to integrate perspectives for a stronger outcome.

8. Evaluate products, experiences, projects, and events to ensure mission satisfaction.

9. Gather and combine human resources to supply needs and lower capital costs.

10. Innovate to differentiate services and compete at a higher level.

SUMMARY

- Work-related skills generally fall into three main categories: technical skills, (which are usually tied to a particular job), personal traits (usually characteristics about you that are stable over your lifetime), and transferable skills (which can be applied to many jobs).

- Transferable skills are the most important to consider when changing jobs, fields, or careers.

- Transferable skills fall into the four quadrants, depending on how much you enjoy using these capabilities and how good you are at them.

- It's most important to know which skills you are great at and which you enjoy using most. Find jobs that depend on those skills.

ACTIVITIES

For groups

In addition to the exercises in this chapter, try some of these activities with a group.

Assign Chapter Six for the group (reading and the exercises). At the next meeting, try the activity below. Have people share their answers with the group one at a time or partner up and have people discuss as a pair.

1) Have each group member share a summary of their top skills, focusing on those they are proficient in and enjoy using most. Ask the rest of the group to give feedback to each person. Do group members see the same skills as the individual? Do they see skills the person can't see within themselves? Have the group brainstorm ideas of jobs that match the skills of each person.

"The whole is greater than the sum of its parts."

ARISTOTLE

CHAPTER SEVEN

Putting It All Together

Wrapping up assessment information and finding additional support

So now you have assessed all aspects of your V.I.N.E.S—Values, Interests, Natural Disposition, Exceptional Qualities, and Skills.

Based on the information you have gathered, what is calling out to you? Use the lists of suggested jobs from formal assessments, your gut feelings, jobs you've dreamed of, and any useful occupational information gathered from your assessment efforts. Using these sources, start a list of possible jobs that are a good match for you.

If you haven't already, consider sharing your results with others you trust and respect. Select people who have your best interests in mind and don't have a hidden agenda. Ask them to help you brainstorm jobs and careers that meet your V.I.N.E.S. Be open to suggestions if you ask for them. Don't judge or shoot things down immediately. Anything that sincerely interests you deserves further research at this point.

To keep your research activities to a reasonable amount of time, narrow down your focus to no more than three job titles. You'll see why in the next chapter—the more options you choose to research, the more work you give yourself. Also, you might overwhelm yourself with too many possibilities. Three will give you options while helping you stay focused. Never put all of your eggs in one basket!

At this point, you want to generate job titles that interest you, match your top values, utilize your strengths, and use skills you are proficient in and enjoy using. It may be hard to find jobs that exactly match all of your criteria, but get as close as you can. Now you have to continue the A.S.T.E.R. Career Model process by exploring, investigating, and testing out options (which we'll explore in PART TWO).

SUMMARY OF YOUR V.I.N.E.S.

Values—my top five work values are the following:

_____

_____

_____

_____

_____

**Interests—list some areas of interest for you
and your Holland Code.**

_____

_____

_____

_____

My Holland Code is: _____ _____ _____

Natural Disposition—write down some of the key aspects of your personality in your own words.

_____

_____

_____

_____

Exceptional Qualities—list some of your superpowers and things you do exceptionally well.

_____

_____

_____

_____

Skills—list the transferable skills you enjoy and excel in the most right now.

_____

_____

_____

_____

List six jobs that could match your values, interests, and personality, and utilize your best transferable skills.

_____

_____

_____

_____

_____

_____

How well does each of these career options fit your V.I.N.E.S.?

_____

_____

_____

_____

_____

_____

List any other jobs you would like to explore.

_____

_____

_____

_____

_____

What research do you need to conduct to know which of these is the best option for you right now?

_____

_____

_____

_____

_____

Who can you talk to or where can you go to learn more about each of these roles?

_____

_____

_____

_____

_____

When will you do this?

_____

_____

_____

_____

_____

How to get more help and a word about career professional credentials

If you are still feeling stuck at this point, try to get some help. Go to your local community college career center, your local workforce development office, or your alma mater career office, or consider hiring a career professional. When hiring a professional, do due diligence to make sure the person is a good match for you. At a minimum, ask about their fees, credentials, the type of clients they work well with, and how their process works. Credentials and quality vary greatly. I love helping individuals and groups with career advising. If you want to learn more about my credentials and services, please go to Brand Career Management at www.brandcareermanagement.com.

It's worth noting that the field of career counseling and coaching does not have any one organization regulating it. Some groups offering credentials include the International Coaching Federation, the National Career Development Association, Career Thought Leaders, and Career Directors International. These organizations have "authority" over their members but not over anyone outside of the organization. They don't have any formal authority to enforce professional standards on the entire profession. Here are a few definitions to help you navigate the sometimes confusing arena of career assistance.

Life coaching: Career coaching is not the same as life coaching. A life coach might help someone with career issues, but that is generally not their specialty. Life coaching takes on a broader array of less tangible topics (such as decision making, building self-esteem, etc.). Credentials can be murky, and this field is not regulated.

Career coaching: This could cover specific topics, such as assessment, job search, branding, and career management. It is more future-focused, trying to meet you where you are to help you move forward. Career coaching is usually concentrated on helping someone with a specific career challenge in a short time frame, although plenty of people seek ongoing career coaching at various stages of their career journey. There is no single definitive authority regulating career coaches. You must do your homework because people can call themselves a career coach without any formal credentials. Career coaches often come from other areas, such as human resources, recruiting, teaching, IT, marketing, etc. This may be a second career for a career coach, and it's not uncommon for someone to become a career coach after going through their own career change. Career coaches are trained to stick to their area of expertise, and it's unethical for them to address mental health issues with you, such as drug addiction, marital conflicts, or ADHD, with you (unless they happen to also be a licensed counselor).

Career counseling: This service may cover the same topics as career coaching, but professionals in this area are usually more skilled in counseling techniques, workplace psychology, and assessments. Career counseling may focus more on the past and figuring out "How did I get here?" before deciding your next steps. Each state in the U.S. has different laws deciding who can call themselves career counselors. In 2015, the National Career Development Association changed its definition of a career counselor to include only people who have some type of master's in counseling. Before this, people with a master's degree in psychology or a related area would qualify. It's interesting to note that this new definition excludes Richard Bolles. He is the author of the legendary career book *What Color Is Your Parachute?* Many people refer to him as the grandfather of modern career counseling. He held a theology master's degree in the New Testament. It also means that the association does not recognize me as a career counselor. However, in the State of Maryland, where I lived for 20+ years,

I was allowed to call myself a career counselor because I have a master's in applied psychology (industrial/organizational). In some states, I would have to be a licensed counselor to call myself a career counselor. Career counselors (unless they happen to also be licensed counselors) must stay in their area of expertise, and it's unethical for them to address mental health issues with you.

Counseling: Also known as therapy or psychotherapy, every state in the U.S. regulates the licensure and behavior of counselors operating in its jurisdiction. Counselor education is extensive, and earning the degree can take a long time. Most counselors have a specialty. Though rare, you can find some who focus on career counseling. The following is a partial list of some focus areas for counselors: marital counseling, mental health, family dynamics, vocational rehabilitation (which is for people seeking jobs/careers after an event has affected their ability to work as before), and addiction. You may want to consider working with a licensed counselor if you have issues outside of career management and you want to address both at the same time.

Career certifications: No matter the level of education of a career professional, many practitioners obtain certifications to supplement formal training and enhance expertise. I know of at least 70, and there are likely hundreds. They often require a test; they always require time and money to obtain, and many require continuing education to keep the certification valid. There is no organization that governs the quality of these programs, and some are more reputable than others.

If you are seeking help for a specific career need, see if the professional has a certification tied to that specialty, and check out the organization that conferred the credential. For example, there are certifications for helping people go through the federal hiring process, so if you seek a U.S. government job, someone with these credentials will know more about federal hiring processes and practices than the average career professional. There are numerous resume certifications with varied levels of difficulty to obtain, so if you seek a resume writer, see if they have any resume certifications. The organization that conferred the credential may share the criteria to obtain it. This may give you some sense of the experience level of the professional.

Workforce development: Every geographic area in the U.S. has a designated workforce development office. They are allocated based on population, so cities often have multiple offices, while rural areas might have one office for multiple counties. The quality of staff at a local workforce office can vary greatly. Also, the level of education and experience of staff may differ by location. One commonality among most of the offices is that the demand for their services can outweigh the availability of staff.

These offices may be run by a state, a county, a non-profit, or some combination of these entities. Services are free, and some offices offer funding to obtain certifications or other workforce training to qualified individuals. Qualifying for services usually means you need to be unemployed, underemployed, or have a low-income household. There are lots of training opportunities funded by the U.S. Department of Labor that are offered at the local level to support workforce needs of local jurisdictions, especially in emerging and in-demand career paths. In past years, I've seen workforce programs designed to train new welders, to bring women into the construction trade, and to provide IT certifications to those with no previous IT experience.

Seek out your local office to see what they have to offer. Workforce development services are often unknown to residents. I worked in my local workforce office for many years, and the one statement I heard the most was "I never knew this resource existed." You can go to Career One Stop at https://www.careeronestop.org/LocalHelp/local-help.aspx and enter your zip code to find the office closest to you.

Career center for a community college or university: Most colleges have a career center, though the level of staffing can range from one person to an entire office. Services are always free to current students. Some colleges offer services free to alumni though there is a trend to charge for these services in cases where there are many alumni, Some community colleges allow local residents to access their career center for free. It's worth looking into your alma mater or local institution to see if you can access quality services, especially if they are free.

After starting out in human resources, Jennifer had fallen into a series of jobs that involved operations and organizational development. She had accumulated almost 10 years of experience running Jewish congregations in Toronto and Washington, D.C. Her last job with a synagogue ended in a tough way. She was let go, mainly due to politics and misunderstandings. She had been looking for a few months with no luck, so she decided to hire some help. When she came to me, she was anxious about finding her next role and concerned about earning her full potential. She had decided that she wanted to explore opportunities outside of the religious arena, but she wasn't sure what else would be a good fit. Jennifer wanted to have a fresh start, so we utilized the A.S.T.E.R. Career Model in order to find her next best option.

We went through the assessment process to clarify her V.I.N.E.S.—Values, Interests, Natural Disposition, Exceptional Qualities, and Skills. We confirmed that her past strengths were still true, but she needed a new environment in which to use them.

Values: Her top values were having honesty and integrity, exercising competence, tackling challenging problems, and working independently. Her values made her realize that she wanted to continue making a positive impact on others. She decided that she wanted to work for a well-respected, non-profit that was large and inclusive.

Interests: Her Holland Code result was E, C, S. Indeed, her past roles required certain qualities: someone with an entrepreneurial mind who enjoys detailed work and helping others and likes to create order in a structured environment. Even though her score on "I" was low in her Holland Code, her personality results demonstrated that she loved problem solving.

Natural Disposition: Jennifer had a hard time deciding which Myers-Briggs type was a better fit, ISTJ or ISTP. Though her results were on the borderline of P vs. J, she confirmed that she preferred a structured and efficient work environment. After validating and discussing the results, we could see themes in her personality that encompassed aspects of both types: being practical and analytical, as well as being friendly, loyal, and reserved.

Exceptional Qualities: Some strengths that came up in multiple assessments were her ability to lead, analyze, and organize while building impactful relationships with others. Her strengths helped her go through the transition process. She took her job search as a problem to be solved and harnessed all of her resources to accomplish the goal. Her analytical skills shined as she made spreadsheets to track job openings, how they matched her V.I.N.E.S., and who she had contacted.

Skills: Some of her top skills were organizing, analyzing, providing excellent customer service, strategizing, and leadership. It was clear that all of her past roles required these skills, she excelled in them, and she wanted to continue using them on a daily basis.

After synthesizing the data and conducting informational interviews, she decided to seek out COO-type roles with local non-profits. These roles offered the best chance to use her transferable skills. Within a few months, she landed a job with a large well-known, non-profit running services for their staff. Interestingly enough, she was my first client to be disappointed with the job offer she landed. Even though it was a large employer with many possible paths within, she wasn't excited about the immediate role. She was concerned about being pigeon-holed because she was only taking on a piece of a COO-type role. She knew she was capable of more and didn't want to hurt any chances of moving into a bigger role down the road.

After helping her negotiate an acceptable salary, I suggested she take the opportunity because she hadn't had any other offers up to that point, and she was worried about long-term loss of income. I pointed out that there was room to grow in such a large organization. Plus, she had shared that her potential future boss and interviewer had said that he planned to retire in the near future. This job offered her a great opportunity to use her best skills and replace her previous income with a very solid organization. I also pointed out that she could keep looking within and outside of the company.

She took the job and within a few months COVID-19 happened. She reached out soon after to share her relief that she had accepted the job. Though there were challenges, she liked working at the employer and was happy to be employed. After COVID-19 forced necessary changes to the delivery of services provided to employees, she strategically solved the problem and had the programs adapted in no time. I'm happy to share that she recently reached out to say that she was able to move up into her boss's role and things are working out well.

SUMMARY

- Pull all of your assessment information together.

- Reflect on the results and see what is speaking to you.

- Share the results with trusted people to see if they have any different insights.

- Create a target list of three job titles for further exploration.

- Seek help from a private practice career professional if you're not able to generate a list of three job titles.

- Remember that there are various levels of career professionals based on credentials.

- Research a few professionals, and pick the one who best suits your needs.

- Consider using other resources, such as local workforce development offices and college career offices.

ACTIVITIES

For individuals

In addition to the exercises in the previous chapters, try to gather more information and confirm results with others. This could be a few close friends or former colleagues. It could happen by meeting individually with people or in a group setting.

For groups

If you have been meeting as a group to go through Chapters Two through Six, assign Chapter Seven for the next meeting. Have attendees share what they think their V.I.N.E.S. are suggesting in terms of job titles to target. Gather feedback from the group. Do they see alignment? Do they have other ideas?

RECOMMENDED RESOURCES

In alphabetical order by author, the following books offer excellent advice on different aspects of job search and career management. Some are written specifically for women.

Nourish Your Career by Shahrzad Arasteh offers a compilation of career advice and recipes from 17 colleagues on all things related to career management.

Women Don't Ask: Negotiation and the Gender Divide co-authored by Linda Babcock is a powerful book that explains why women lose potential income over the course of their careers. It also offers advice on how to ask and why women should always try to negotiate their salaries.

Feminist Fight Club by Jessica Bennett is a creatively designed book that helps women nagivate unpleasant situations that come up at work. It suggests practical advice that can be implemented right away. Though the topic is serious, the book will make you smile.

eParachute, found at https://eparachute.com/, is a web platform co-founded by Richard Bolles's son Gary Bolles. It takes the concepts from the original book *What Color is Your Parachute?* and brings them to life in a virtually interactive platform.

What Color Is Your Parachute? by Richard Bolles is considered "the Bible" of job search and has been updated regularly since it was first written. Sadly, Richard Bolles died in 2017 after finalizing the 2018 edition. Thankfully, his words will live on forever.

Dorie Clark has written four books, and all of them can improve your career management efforts in different ways. Her first book, *Reinventing You,* focuses on understanding your strengths and creating your personal brand. *Stand Out* offers advice on becoming a thought leader and making an impact on the world. *Entrepreneurial You* gives practical guidance on making a viable income as a self-employed businessperson. Dorie's latest book, *The Long Game,* offers direction on a variety of career management topics, including long-term strategies for goal setting, life design, networking, branding, and time management.

Help Wanted: An A to Z Guide to Cope with the Ups and Downs of the Job Search by Karen Litzinger is a motivational and powerful new publication designed for job seekers who may be struggling to stay positive.

Bring Your Brain to Work by Professor Art Markman offers a scientific approach based on the latest research. His book addresses job search, succeeding at work, and finding your next role, and it provides actionable advice backed by cognitive science.

A Woman's Guide to Successful Negotiating: How to Convince, Collaborate, & Create Your Way to Agreement by Lee Miller and his daughter Jessica offers a framework to utilize for all types of negotiations. Though only one chapter is specific to salary negotiation, the book shares many ideas on ways women can leverage their strengths when negotiating.

"All sorts of things can happen when you're open to new ideas and playing around with things."

STEPHANIE KWOLEK, CHEMIST WHO INVENTED
KEVLAR AND WINNER OF THE LAVOISIER MEDAL
FOR TECHNICAL ACHIEVEMENTS

PART TWO

INVESTIGATION

After completing PART ONE, you now have a few job titles to explore. This brings you to the "S" and "T" parts of the A.S.T.E.R. Career Model where you seek additional information and test out options.

"The best way to leapfrog in your career is to get advice from someone who's done what you're trying to accomplish. It helps clear all the doubt."

HEATHER ANNE CARSON, CO-FOUNDER, REPABLE

CHAPTER EIGHT

Seek Out Information

After you have given thoughtful consideration to your V.I.N.E.S. and gathered career options to explore, you need to do research! You can do this by reading information, talking to others, and finding ways to "test the idea." A combination of all three is optimal for your strategic exploration.

At this point in your initial research, there are three important items to learn about in regards to each possible career path:

1) **Can you make enough money to live the life you want in this job/career (now or in the future)?** Of course, this requires you to know how much money you need annually, so you may need to create a budget to estimate your current financial needs.

2) **Do you have the skills and education needed to qualify for this role (or do you have the access, time, and money to obtain the necessary credentials)?** If you don't, you can look into time and costs for necessary training and factor that into your decision-making process.

3) **Is this job/field growing, shrinking, or stable?** As you would imagine, some fields like IT and healthcare are going gangbusters, while other industries, like manufacturing, are slowing. If an industry is slowing or stagnant, it will be harder to find a job because there are fewer of them. If the job is in high demand, there will be more opportunities but also more competition. Your geographic location might be a magnet or headquarters for certain businesses. New York and Los Angeles are centers for the media industry. Silicon Valley and Austin, TX, are

known for jobs in technology. Charlotte, NC, is home to many bank headquarters, and Montgomery County, MD, is a hotbed for the gaming industry. Consider if you are willing to move in order to be in a robust place for your target job/industry. Finally, as we have seen firsthand, unpredictable circumstances, such as a pandemic or a natural disaster, can change the demand for an industry overnight.

The answers to these three questions are easy to find. You can find this type of information using books or online resources designed for this purpose. The U.S. Department of Labor has multiple free websites and resources. Much of the data originates from the Bureau of Labor Statistics, which then distributes it in a variety of formats, including websites and publications. I caution you: The Department of Labor is making predictions based on data and they aren't always correct. Their data will never be in real time. That is why it's also good to talk to a person doing the work to gather the most up-to-date information.

Occupational research resources

Two free online resources from the Department of Labor are My Next Move at www.mynextmove.org and O*NET at https://www.onetonline.org/.

My Next Move provides assessments and career exploration information to help people considering a career change.

O*NET offers a wealth of career information, including detailed descriptions for thousands of jobs (such as income range, education required, and job demand). It provides a variety of ways to search for jobs (such as by interests, skills, abilities, and industry). It also allows you to "crosswalk" to other career resources, so you can align codes previously obtained from the Military Occupational Classification, the *Occupational Outlook Handbook*, and the Dictionary of Occupational Titles. O*NET is basically the online version of the *Occupational Outlook Handbook*.

Although job posting sites (such as CareerBuilder, Indeed, and Monster) are the worst way to land a job, they can be a good way to verify the reality of the information from these government career sites. Department of Labor predictions might be off (because they are making predictions about the future), but job boards and networking can give you real-time data about salaries and educational requirements.

The Bureau of Labor Statistics publishes resources that you can find in a library (such as the *Occupational Outlook Handbook*). Also, there are many published career books on specific occupations and industries. Look for them in educational settings, workforce offices, and libraries, and on Amazon.

After performing this research, you might be able to rule out some of the jobs you were considering and narrow your focus. The next level of research would be talking to people who do this work. This is a critical part of your exploration! The previous research gets you the initial information to make some decisions, but O*NET doesn't tell you everything. For example, it doesn't share that it would be very difficult for an ER nurse to do her job well if she faints every time she sees blood. Finding out this kind of information is best done by talking to others who do this work on a daily basis. Vetting a job or career path by using both forms of research will lessen the chance of making a decision based on incomplete or outdated information.

Informational interviews

Informational interviews are one of the best ways to discover more about a job or career path. This involves reaching out to people who do the work you think you want to do. When you meet, virtually or in person, you will ask questions to uncover information that will help you make decisions about which path you will pursue. It's always best to try to meet in person because it's easier to make a human connection that way. However, due to COVID-19 and other possible limitations, you may need to meet by phone or through an online platform such as Zoom. Regardless of the setting, it's acceptable to ask for 20 to 30 minutes. Be respectful by sticking to the agreed upon time frame.

How do you find these people? This is the most common question I hear about this topic. There is no silver bullet answer. As crazy as it might sound, ask everyone you know if they know someone who does that job or someone who works for a target company. This is helpful because it could lead to a warm contact and someone who can make an introduction. However, sometimes you may have to seek out a stranger, make a cold call, or send an email to someone who you have never met.

When I ran my first set of informational interviews in the 90s, I used a phone book to find the interviewees. These days, I would suggest using the internet and social media. You can search using keywords to find people working in a certain industry, at a specific company, or in a geographic area that interests you. On LinkedIn, you can type the name of a company to see if you have connections to anyone who works or worked there. I am not a big fan of Facebook, but this is the type of activity where that site could help. You could post to all of your Facebook friends to ask, "Does anyone know someone who works at company X? I am trying to find out more by speaking with an internal employee." A friend of mine, who is an avid Facebook user, tried this and received many excellent leads. With diligent follow-up, these leads turned into interviews and three competing job offers.

Here are some strategic tips for informational interviews. You don't have to speak to the highest level person. In fact, the more well-known the person you seek out, the harder it will be to get to speak with them. That said, the worst they can say is no. Persistence and patience sometimes pay off. You should move to another person if you try twice and don't receive any reply. I always say to try two times because the first time you try, your message may get lost in the shuffle of life.

If you reach out to 10 people, expect that a third may not respond, a third may say yes but not follow through, and a third will say yes and be happy to meet with you. If you have a better response rate, good for you! What I'm saying is that some people WILL say yes, so don't be afraid to try. Some people won't reply, but don't let that discourage you. People like to talk about themselves. I promise you will find people if you put in the effort.

You may need to convince some skeptics to meet with you. Informational interviews have been around a while, and along the way some people have abused them. Those people are really asking for a job, but they disguise it as gathering information. Once the meeting starts, people can see right through this, so don't do it. It will make a bad impression.

Early in my career, when I was conducting informational interviews, I came across one person who was suspicious of my intentions. I found him by going through the phone book looking for large, local companies. I would call the HR office and ask to speak with a recruiter. This gentleman was a recruiter at Westinghouse. He said something like, "I really don't have time for this," and it was obvious he thought I was pulling a ruse. I calmly and politely explained that I had recently read *What Color Is Your Parachute?*, done a series of assessments and informational interviews, and now I was trying to narrow down what area of HR I wanted to pursue. That seemed to be enough proof of my serious intentions, and he agreed to meet me. Funny enough, many years later, I ran into him. He was still at the same company, but now it's called Northrop Grumman. He was manning a booth at a job fair with my workforce development employer. I wasn't 100% sure it was him, but when I went home, I found a copy of my notes and realized it was in fact the very same man. This is a good lesson that you never know who might pop up in your future path, so never burn a bridge.

Don't forget to say thanks to those who have helped you. People are giving their time, so you need to show appreciation. If you are meeting in person at a food establishment, it would be classy to pay for the person's food and drink. It's very important to thank the people who meet with you. You can do this by email or mail. Usually, you won't have access to their cell phone, and texting might be too informal for a new acquaintance. Sharing thanks is courteous, and it will make a good impression. We remember people who thank us for what we do, and we also remember those who don't.

In case you are wondering, informational interviews do count as networking because you are growing the number of people who are aware you exist. Also, if you meet with someone and get along well, that person can be a valuable resource if you go into the same field. You can stay in touch and ask them to share future job leads. If you made a good impression, the person will be happy to share posting and insider knowledge.

If you only have a few minutes to speak with someone, the most telling questions to ask are "What do you like most about your job?" and "What do you like least about your job?" You should not inquire about their salary. That is too personal a topic for you to broach, unless you know the person well and know they won't feel uncomfortable with you asking. Instead, try to find compensation information from other sources. Here are a few reputable websites to find salary information: O*NET Online at https://www.onetonline.org/or Salary.com at https://www.salary.com/. Payscale.com at https://www.payscale.com/ includes international data. Glassdoor.com at https://www.glassdoor.com/index.htm offers an unrelated but useful feature of anonymous employer reviews. As a side note, I wouldn't avoid an employer with one or two bad reviews, but if there is an overall negative trend, I would suggest steering away from that employer. With outliers, one disgruntled employee may have a personal agenda, and anonymity can create an atmosphere that encourages sharing of unverifiable comments.

Below is a list of suggested questions you can ask when meeting with others to learn more about a job. You can adapt these questions to learn more about a career, an industry, or a specific employer.

Possible questions to ask in an informational interview

What career path did you follow to get into your current position (companies, jobs, mentors, etc.)?

What is a typical day/week like?

What do you like most about your job?

What do you like least about your job?

What skills, qualities, and/or education are necessary for this type of work?

What is your opinion about the employment outlook for this occupation/field in the next few years? Also, do you recommend any specific publications, websites, or other resources to learn about this industry?

How could someone with my background get into this occupation/field/company?

Are you a member of and/or do you recommend any professional associations or organizations related to this profession? Is there a local chapter? Do you know how I can find out more information?

Can you refer me to any other individuals in this field who might be helpful for further information?

You should always meet with at least two people who do the job you are researching because it's best not to make a major career decision based on only one person's opinion. You might meet with someone who is new to the field and isn't yet aware of the major pitfalls of the job. On the other hand, you might meet with someone who has burned out of a role and has a very jaded perspective. You might also meet with someone who had a bad boss, is fulfilling a parent's career dream, or was unfairly treated in a workplace, and now that person has blamed the job itself for the dissatisfaction (when in reality there are other factors influencing her perspective). Given the possible pitfalls associated with only speaking with one person in your prospective field, you need to get a broader view of things to make an informed decision. Taking the advice of one person and acting on it could steer you toward or away from something based on limited information.

By doing your research and talking to others, you are trying to find out if this particular role is the right move for you. You are trying to further validate if it is a good fit based on your V.I.N.E.S. (Values, Interests, Natural Abilities, Exceptional Qualities, and Skills), along with the three initial questions related to income potential, required education, and industry growth.

Once you have gone through this process, one of the following will be true:

1. You have discovered a good match or two (three titles are acceptable to target if they are in related fields: for example, accounting, bookkeeping, and auditing). Other than that, you will get distracted trying to chase too many targets. Now that you have a manageable number of targets, you can move to the next step of testing out options or going right into planning and executing your job search campaign.

2. You have ruled out all of the options you researched for one reason or another. If so, you will need to go back and explore more. Find a few more titles that matched most of your criteria but that you decided not to pursue the first go around (e.g., your fourth, fifth, and sixth choices).

3. You still feel confused. If you are still unsure at this point, you may want to hire someone to help you figure out what is preventing you from moving forward.

It's okay to choose to move forward with something that's not a 100% fit as long as you go into it with open eyes and know where you might get stuck or hit roadblocks and you're willing to stand up to those potential barriers.

For example, if you go into a traditionally male field like programming, construction, or production, you will likely face gender discrimination. In these cases, if you have the strength and personality to not be bothered by others' biases, you might want to continue to pursue work in these fields.

You may be very interested in a job that involves a lot of paperwork, but you learned from your assessment phase that you really don't enjoy paperwork and you tend to put it off. Assuming the rest of the job fits you very well, you might accept this job knowing that you must have discipline in setting aside time regularly to perform that task. You will need to keep on top of this so it doesn't build up and frustrate you. You might also ask targeted questions in your informational interviews about how much paperwork is really involved, how much time it takes on average, etc.

An important part of your research is about finding (and filling) any potential gaps. These might be gaps in education, training, or your knowledge of the industry. Once you pinpoint potential areas for development, look into resources to help you get up to speed. This could include professional development opportunities inside or outside of a company. In addition, seek out possible mentors in the field and industry-related associations. Professional associations are a rich source of networking and learning opportunities.

I can't emphasize enough the importance of doing research before making a career decision. If you are unsure of where to go next in your career, speaking to others who do that work will be invaluable. In the beginning of the process, you may use informational interviews to reduce the number of your job targets. Later in the process, you may use it to narrow down a position within a field or to uncover employers who match your values.

Informational interviews have helped me make informed career decisions many times over the last 20 years. After being laid off from my first "real" job after college, I went through the A.S.T.E.R. Career Model process. During the research phase, the first set of jobs I investigated included volunteer coordinator, institutional research, and human resources. I knocked out the first two options after talking to people in those roles. The research role seemed too solitary. In most colleges, this was a department of one. The volunteer coordinator seemed all-consuming. One person I interviewed was so busy that we had to meet over the phone, and it sounded like that job could take over your life if you let it.

After the first series of informational interviews, I narrowed down my target to HR, but I had also learned that HR is very broad. Unless I wanted to go for a generalist position, I would have to choose an area of focus. Within HR, you can specialize in compensation, training, benefits, employee relations, or recruitment. I conducted a second set of interviews with people in each of these roles to narrow down my target. After gathering enough information, I decided to go for a training role, which turned out to be a great fit. I still train today, and I learned so much from that first job in HR.

SUMMARY

- Once you have some potential job titles to explore, you need to seek out more information to ensure a good fit.

- The most important factors to consider are the expected income, the demand for this job in your location, and your qualifications to do this job in the near future.

- You can perform a lot of useful research online, but eventually you will want to talk to people who do the jobs you are considering.

ACTIVITIES

For individuals

Through research, narrow down your career options to three choices that will allow you to earn what you need to live and are in demand where you live. Also, ensure you have the qualifications to do this job now or have a plan to gain the experience or education needed to fulfill this role.

If you haven't done so already, research three jobs by speaking to two people who do that job right now. If you have a target company in mind, try to find someone who works there or worked there. Look on LinkedIn, and ask people you know.

If you are part of a social or job seekers group, ask people in that group if they know of others you could speak with for informational interviews.

"The price of inaction is far greater than the cost of a mistake."

MEG WHITMAN, FIRST FEMALE TO RUN TWO LARGE U.S. PUBLIC COMPANIES, EBAY AND HP

CHAPTER NINE

Test Assumptions And Explore

Now that you think you know what you want to do, take the plunge and give your new career goal a trial run. After doing the research and informational interviews, testing your assumptions is a great way to further mitigate the chances of making a bad career move. You can do this in many ways, such as volunteering, internships, job shadowing, formal training programs, and taking a temporary job. Additionally, if you are working full time, you could look for opportunities to test out new roles within your company. This can often happen through rotation exercises, cross-training, or a temporary developmental assignment. Even starting a business on the side is a form of exploration.

Caveats: Keep in mind that some employers will be off-limits for testing out a role. In high security environments, such as the National Security Agency or the Federal Bureau of Investigation, you'll need to find a formal experience, such as an internship or training program, to see what it's like to work there.

Apprenticeships can be seen as a way to test drive a job, but they are more akin to starting on a new career path because they usually require a multi-year commitment. You often see apprenticeships in occupations such as plumbing, welding, and carpentry. However, a resurgence of this type of training was expanding these kinds of programs beyond the trades before March 2020. We will see where things go as time passes.

Volunteering

One way to test out an occupation is volunteering to get the experience. This can give you a taste for the work while also giving you experience to put on your resume. Many organizations rely on volunteers to get work done. If you can find a non-profit or community service that needs the skill you are trying to use, offer to volunteer and see what happens. If you don't hear back, then make sure to follow up at least once. This is a non-threatening way to try things out. Often, if it's a good fit, it could turn into a paid position, but even if it doesn't, the experience can be priceless. The nice thing about volunteering is that it's less of a commitment than getting hired, and you can quit more easily if things aren't working out.

Volunteering while unemployed provides multiple benefits. It can help you with transitioning back into a regular schedule and by providing an answer when interviewers ask how you have been spending your free time. If your volunteer work is tied to your profession or industry, it can provide a placeholder on your resume or LinkedIn profile to show current activity. I've seen many examples of someone volunteering and it turning into a job. When you volunteer, people get to know you and what you can do. Being within the organization provides insider knowledge of upcoming job openings and lets you see if it's a place you really want to pursue for employment. I've seen this happen many times, especially within small organizations where volunteering can provide interaction with decision makers. In one great example, a woman who had been volunteering for a religious organization over many years became the CEO of that foundation. She was clearly devoted to their cause and contributed so much that the leader who was about to retire started to groom her as his replacement.

Internships, midternships, and returnships for women

Many people complete internships during undergraduate and graduate studies. These opportunities can be a powerful way to build experience for your resume, give you a taste of what the job or company is like, grow your network, and make a good impression on others in a work setting. During COVID-19, most traditional, in-person internships had to adapt to the virtual world. As with most things, face-to-face internships usually provide a richer experience. However, with the world of work changing to adopt more remote options, virtual internships are probably not going to go away.

Now, there are modern spin offs of this practice for those outside of school called midternships and returnships, which may be paid or unpaid. Midternship is a term for post-graduate and/or mid-career professionals seeking to explore a new field or job. Returnships are another trend that offer on-the-job experience to women re-entering the workforce after an extended time away from it. When returnships started pre-COVID-19, you would see them in certain industries, such as finance, law, and technical fields, but they may become more widespread post-COVID-19.

Non-profit organizations are offering returnships. They work with employers to create opportunities and with mothers who want to get back into their field of work. A few examples are Reboot Accel at https://www.RebootAccel.com (based near San Francisco and focusing on jobs in technology, legal, and finance) and The Mom Project at http://www.themomproject.com out of Chicago. Some for-profit companies are focused on matching women returning to work with flexible employment opportunities. Examples of these are WrK at https://wrk.co and MomCorp at https://www.corpsteam.com/. These are not returnships, but they target a similar audience.

Job shadowing

Another way to gain more in-depth knowledge about a job is to seek out a job shadowing assignment. Just like it sounds, you ask someone doing the job if you could shadow her for a day. This can be a great way to see what the job is like on a day-to-day basis. Of course, this is not possible in some roles. Jobs that require confidentiality, such as human resources and accounting or any patient work in healthcare, will probably not be possible. Also, during a pandemic, following someone in person may not be possible. That said, there are many jobs you can shadow, so give this consideration. When seeking these types of opportunities, it's helpful to ask folks within your network. It won't be as scary to an employer to let you job shadow if someone in the company can vouch for you.

Joanna's story

A childhood friend of mine used job shadowing as a method to modify her career path. She was a sales manager for an event management company for three years before taking time off to raise a family. When she wanted to re-enter the workforce, she took stock and realized she liked sales but didn't want to go back into event management.

She knew someone who was in pharmaceutical sales and asked if she could shadow her for a day. She had a great time and thought, "I can't believe I could make good money doing something that is so much fun." She set her sights on entering that field (applying her transferable skill of selling) and has been very successful in that industry for 14 years.

Formal training and retraining programs

Some companies have robust training programs, which offer a great way to test out a new path in a safe environment. Enterprise Car Rental is well-known for its management training program. Large retail outfits sometimes offer these types of programs, too. Drugstore chains often have training programs for managers and pharmacy technicians. They usually offer extensive training within a short period of time with the goal of having you move into a role where you can work in a location among their chain. Many require a commitment to work for the sponsoring employer for a period of time after the training period ends. Even if you don't stay at the company too long, they can offer great leadership training for your future career.

In recent years, an innovative retraining program came about within the finance industry. Wall Street companies created the Return to Bay Street Award Program to ease women back into their former finance careers. Employers have realized that there is a lot of talent among this group, and they are experiencing a talent shortage, so it makes a lot of sense. I hope to see more of this type of formal training. It's a win-win for the participating employers and former employees.

You can also find industry-specific training programs run outside of companies. Some of which receive funding through workforce development grants (within the U.S., you can use America's Service Locator to enter your zip code and find your closest one-stop career center at https://www.servicelocator.org/StateWebDirectory.asp). These centers are your tax dollars at work, and their programs typically focus on industries that need workers locally.

Some training programs receive funding from non-profits and are tied to certain industries, often a partnership between an educational school and local employers. One example of this is the Ada Developers Academy (ADA) based in Seattle. They work with local powerhouse companies like Amazon, Google, and Microsoft. My niece attended this free program that requires a competitive process to enter.

Tamara's story

With a bachelor's in biology, Tamara was working as a research scientist in a lab conducting technical and analytical work. She was getting bored of the work and wondering about other options. Looking at the other employees around her, most of the roles seemed like something she didn't want to do for the long-term. She saw graduate students and professors who were successful, but it seemed like a hard career path because it was very dependent on grant funding. She had several colleagues who worked as software engineers in the lab. In time, she realized that their work was more stable and interesting, so she decided to learn more about that career path.

My niece took time to look at her V.I.N.E.S. Looking at her personality, her preference for introversion supported a job that provided quiet time for "heads down" work, and her preference for perceiving suggested she appreciated a variety of tasks and a less structured environment. Her interest in science, using data, and performing detail-oriented work implied that she might stay in a STEM field but apply her skills in a different way. Even though she didn't have school debt thanks to scholarships, she realized she would need to make a higher income to have the life she envisioned. She conducted the career exploration process and considered paths like medical school but ultimately decided that computer programming would be a good fit.

Her next challenge was to find training. There were many bootcamps that she could pay for, but she found one that was free. She applied to ADA, which aims itself at female career changers. ADA didn't accept her on her first try, but she was confident in her choice. She reapplied the following year and gained admission to the program. She enjoyed her time in the program, learned from the required internship, and was hired right out of the program. She has been a software developer with GoDaddy for three years and has not had any regrets about her new path.

Finding opportunities within your current company

If you are already working in a job and you enjoy that company, before going outside, see if your next desired job exists inside your organization. Sometimes, staying with the same employer can pay off with benefits, such as gaining seniority, a higher matching percentage for a retirement plan, or more vacation time. If you work at a large enough company, it's possible there are other avenues available for you to find satisfying work.

This situation can be a win-win for you and the organization. From the company's perspective, if you are a valued employee, they will want to keep you and it's less risky to let you try a new role than to hire a completely unknown person. If they know you are unhappy in your current role and they know another role at the company would be a good fit, they may be willing to let you test that out.

There are many ways to go about searching for new roles with your current employer. You could manage this transition by taking on some duties of the new role (while keeping your current role) or arrange it so that your job becomes 50% of the old and 50% of the new. You could be cross-trained in a new role while you stay in your current role. You could also ask to go fulltime into a new role for a trial period. This allows you and the employer to see how it might work out before fully committing to this path. You could ask your employer to ensure the ability to go back to your old role if it doesn't work out. If a coworker is going to be out for a while (on maternity leave or FMLA), you can ask to fill the role while she is gone. You could also ask the incumbent to allow you to shadow for a day. As you can see, when you are creative and your employer is accommodating, there are many ways to test out options while staying within a great company.

Temporary work

Finally, going through a temporary agency or finding short-term assignments can be a way to test out a new role. Temporary agencies can offer you a glimpse of what it's like to work in certain companies or industries without you having to commit to any one job for a long time.

With some types of work, you won't be hired without experience, but there are some times when no experience is necessary or employers are willing to train you. This can happen when a company needs a lot of workers for a short period of time. One example would be a movie production that needs hundreds of extras for certain scenes over the course of a month. Or a company might need to hire 100 people for three months and expects to have to train all of them, such as when selling a new product during the holidays.

Entrepreneurship

If entrepreneurship interests you, give it a test run while you are working full time. This is a great way to test your level of interest and commitment (because it will be hard doing two jobs at once) and to test the viability of your idea. You will get to research, test the market, and feel like an entrepreneur while still having the stable income from your current work.

This is what I did, and it did pay off. From 2011 to 2015, I worked fulltime in workforce development while starting and growing my business. It was hard work, but this busy time proved to me that there was a market for my career counseling services, and I loved being an entrepreneur enough to do it fulltime.

If you are interested in more information on entrepreneurship as a new path, there are more details and resources mentioned in the next chapter.

SUMMARY

- Testing out a role before fully committing to it can be a great way to avoid a bad fit.

- Trying out roles using methods like volunteering, job shadowing, formal training programs, and taking a temporary job allow you to test drive before making a full career pivot.

- Considering opportunities within your current company or becoming an entrepreneur as a side gig are both ways to maintain some stable income while experimenting.

ACTIVITIES

For groups

1) Have each person take time to reflect on a future desired role. Have attendees write down possible titles and potential ways to test out these new roles.

2) Have each person share their answers. Ask the group to brainstorm additional ways to test out specific roles. Ask each group member if they know someone who can help connect the person to someone else for more assistance.

"It takes as much energy to wish as it does to plan."

ELEANOR ROOSEVELT

PART THREE

IMPLEMENTATION

"Dreams are lovely but they are just dreams. Fleeting, ephemeral, pretty. But dreams do not come true just because you dream them. It's hard work that makes things happen. It's hard work that creates change."

SHONDA RHIMES, CREATIVE/EXECUTIVE PRODUCER, GREY'S ANATOMY AND SCANDAL

CHAPTER TEN

Execute Your Career Plan

Getting the role you want

You've gone through the hard work and now you have found a career direction. It's likely one of the following (or a combination of them):

1) Develop in place (stay in your current job or company but change/add/shed some responsibilities and challenges).

2) Start your own business.

3) Get a new job (change jobs or get back in the workforce).

No matter your goal, you will need these four things: goal setting, structure, time management, and networking.

Goal setting

Now you need to execute a plan to make it happen. Depending on your path, the steps will differ. No matter which path you choose, you will want to create some daily structure and lay out your end goal(s). Then, break each large goal into smaller steps and give yourself some deadlines for completion.

Write down your long-term goal(s), and display them in a place you see often. Evaluate periodically to see if you are on track or need to make adjustments. You can set your goals in a formal way (draw up a business plan) or more loosely (write them down in a diary or create a mind map). One way or another, have a clear vision of the result you want and the steps needed to get there. Then get started.

Structure

If you have lost a job and are trying to get a new one, be sure to recreate structure. Don't underestimate the power of a schedule and the difficulty of losing a familiar routine. Most of us have predictable patterns of energy in our daily lives. Figure out what time of day is the most energetic for you and plan to tackle your toughest tasks during those time frames. To extroverts, networking can seem like fun, so maybe filling out a job application is your toughest task. For introverts, networking activities may be the toughest, so plan accordingly. Do what works best for you, but do build regularity into your schedule of tasks. Set norms. For example, "Each morning from 10 to 11a.m. I will make cold calls." Set quotas. For example, "I will have two networking meetings per week." Then, work the plan. In job search, you are creating a structure of time that is temporary because once you land your next job, your routine will change again.

If you are planning to start a business, you still need to create structure. However, in this case, you want to create a sustainable routine that can become part of your business model. Start by sketching out an ideal work week that suits your lifestyle. Schedule your toughest business activities during your most productive times of day.

Let me suggest a tip I learned from my esteemed colleague, Karen Chopra, when I was starting out as an entrepreneur. If you'd like to see five clients a week, set aside time for that, even if you don't have any clients yet. Until you have clients, you can use that time to work on marketing to gain clients. This will get you into a routine to dedicate that time to servicing clients. Once your client list fills up, you will need to find other times for marketing. That is okay, and it is a beneficial modification as your business grows.

This method helps you proactively set your structure, rather than reactively scheduling what comes your way. Usually, when we are reactive versus proactive, we are letting others determine our schedule. Of course, when starting out, sometimes you need to accommodate the clients' time frames, but it's best to start with your ideal structure in mind and to strive for that as much as possible.

In terms of your personality, you may have more preference for structure. As you may recall from Chapter Four, a person who has a personality type that contains the letter "J" thrives under a regular schedule and clear expectations. If this is the case for you, creating structure will be productive, comforting, and motivating. If your preference was for less structure (people with the letter "P" in their personality type prefer fewer restraints), you may feel stifled by a schedule, but it will be important to keep you honest about how you spend your time. Consider giving yourself one day a week to have no plan; you can be spontaneous and do whatever moves you that day.

Time management

Time management is an important part of achieving your goals. Any goal worth chasing will require effort and energy. You need to protect each minute and be true to yourself by setting a realistic amount of time to implement your plan.

Some time management tips:

- Create structure to help you use time more efficiently.

- Be realistic about how long things will take.

- Learn to say no to things that don't align with your end goal.

- Do the hardest thing first. When there is something you don't want to do, make yourself spend some time on it first thing in the morning. Try this and tell me if you don't feel very accomplished within the first few hours of being awake.

- Always make time for those tasks that are important but not urgent, even if you are just tackling them little by little.

Recommended reading

7 Habits of Highly Effective People by Stephen Covey is an excellent book to learn more about goal setting, structure, and time management. It offers a framework to create structure in your life to focus on the things that matter most to you.

Start Finishing: How to Go from Idea to Done by Charlie Gilkey is a great book on project management. It offers a framework to help you start and, more importantly, to finish projects, regardless of size. His time management insights are invaluable.

Networking

Regardless of which route you choose, you will need to network, which means developing and growing professional relationships. Your end goal will determine the types of people you network with and places where you should be networking (i.e., a job seeker may attend an industry job fair, whereas an entrepreneur may join a business referral group). The last chapter of this book goes into detail on networking.

Developing in place

Another option besides finding a new job or starting a business is to develop in place. This means you stay at your job but something changes. You might take on a new responsibility, learn a new skill, change locations, join a new team, shadow a coworker, or volunteer for an additional assignment separate from your regular job (i.e., a stretch assignment). You might learn from a new experience, participate in cross-training, or apply for an in-house training (a management trainee or leadership program). It's possible that you teach yourself a new skill or volunteer to learn it outside of work. Maybe seeking out a mentor in your field can help you grow.

The concept of developing in place is useful if you love your employer, your team, your boss, or all of the above. Sometimes, you need a change in the skills you are using. If you have been doing the same job with the same responsibilities, you will likely get bored or burnout. Usually, making a change in your role or duties will give you a different experience, which can allow you to grow and develop, while keeping the stability of your income and staying with a good employer.

Entrepreneurship

If you've decided you're going to try entrepreneurship, I have a few tips for you on the beginning steps.

First of all, it's worth testing the waters while you are still working full time. This is the safest strategy, especially if your income is essential. It can take time to execute the many steps one must take, such as deciding on a business name, establishing an online presence, getting a logo, etc. It can be helpful to take care of these items slowly while you are still working and have an income. Then, you'll be able to start up faster once you make the full leap.

If you can or must go full swing into it, be patient with yourself. These developments take time, but try to find your focus or niche (on the product/services or clients), as fast as you can. Aim to start bringing in clients

ASAP, and plan out your finances to know the timeline available to establish a successful business or when you must decide to go another route.

One final note about entrepreneurship: It's not for everyone! If you are not self-disciplined, willing to play many roles in the beginning, get lonely easily, and don't like being in charge, this experience may not be for you. Or maybe you need a more stable income. That's one more sign that this may not be the time to start a business. Like most things in life, demand for your products and services seems to come in waves and sometimes they are hard to ride. Within a year, you may have some extreme highs and lows. Over the years, you want to see progression. Did you make more this year than last year?

You should do thorough research before jumping into entrepreneurship. There are a few ways to explore this option:

Assessments: One assessment to identify your innate strengths and challenges is the Entrepreneurial Style and Success Indicator by CRG. You can take this assessment online for a fee on the CRGleader website at https://crgleader.com/entreprenurial-style-and-success-indicator/.

Research: Talk to others who run their own businesses in the same industry. Most will be happy to speak with you (especially those who see you as "coopetition"), but, just to be safe, seek out others outside of your immediate geographic area because those who believe in a scarcity mentality (as opposed to an abundant mind-set) may not speak with you because they only see you as competition.

Test the waters: Why not start a side gig while you work fulltime? This allows you to get your feet wet earning more income without losing the stability of your job. You will be very busy trying to do a full-time and part-time job, but if you really want to become an entrepreneur, it's a very practical way to get started, and with today's portfolio career being a norm, what do you have to lose?

Resources: For a free resource, utilize your local Senior Corps of Retired Executives (SCORE) office, which is tied to the Small Business Administration. Most SCORE offices offer a mix of free individual business coaching with workshops on business topics for a nominal fee. They will ask you questions like those that follow. These are important questions to answer before you invest significant time and money into any business. If you don't have reasonable answers to these questions, it's best to hold off starting the business until you have them.

SCORE will also recommend that you create a business plan as a first step. The questions below will help with filling in your business plan. Even if you divert from the plan later, it is worth the time and energy to map out some basic information to keep you focused and motivated early on.

If you can afford it, consider hiring a business coach to keep you on track. There are different types of business coaches. To find one, you can run a Google search and read the reviews and testimonials. I suggest seeking out recommendations. Inquire with colleagues you respect who have worked with a business coach. Ask them about their experience, and if appropriate, ask for contact information. Figure out where you need the most help to hire the right one. Some will be industry-specific; some will focus on data and stats; some coaches gear themselves toward establishing a new business; most will focus on growing your business.

Down the road, you might also consider hiring someone to help you get up and running on needed software programs (QuickBooks or a customer relationship management system such as Infusionsoft or Salesforce). Outsourcing administrative tasks to a virtual assistant or contracting IT assistance for newsletters and websites can help you focus more on what you love to do. As you grow, consider outsourcing what you hate doing so you can focus on what you love to do within your business.

Questions to answer before starting a business

What is the product or service you plan to provide?

Who needs it? (How old are they, what do they do, what do they read, where do they hang out, etc.) The clearer you are on this, the better!

What will be the benefits to those customers/clients?

Do a SWOT analysis: strengths (yours and your business's), weaknesses (yours and your business's), opportunities (how will you get new clients?), and threats (who is your competition?).

Identify and research potential competitors. How do they price? What do they offer? How does your product/service differ from theirs? What are the advantages/disadvantages of your product or service to theirs?

How does your experience prepare you for this new venture?

Are you planning to do this full time or as a side gig?

How much time do you have to do the work it will take to establish this business (on a daily, weekly, or monthly basis)?

How long can you last without earning any money? Is that enough time to establish your business?

Do you have money to invest in the business? How much?

Do you need upfront money for equipment or other startup costs? If needed, would you qualify for a business loan? Are you willing to take on debt? How do you plan to pay off the loan?

Personally, I recommend being very conservative when beginning the business in terms of money. I would try to use as much of your own time and expertise, until you start bringing in income to use to build the business. Also think about bartering or other ways you can be creative about gathering startup resources.

So, you're going to move forward...

Once you've found satisfactory answers to those questions, you may decide to move forward with establishing your business. Now you need to figure out the legal status you want: sole proprietor, limited liability (LLC), S corporation, C corporation, or partnership. There are pros and cons to each. Your business goals and applicable tax laws will help you determine which one is best for you. You can do some basic research online, but ultimately consulting with a CPA and/or an attorney who knows your line of business will be worth the investment when making this decision. Make sure you seek out professionals who are familiar with the laws where you plan to operate your business.

Next, you'll want to decide on a business name, get an Employer Identification Number (EIN), and open a bank account. Plan out a budget for the first two to three years, based on your research.

Handle necessary formalities, such as registering your business if required in your location. Check local, county, state, and federal laws that apply to you and your business—such as tax laws, licensing, or zoning. If needed, register a trade name, or look into patenting.

You may need some of the same marketing materials as a job seeker (business cards, a resume, and a bio for proposals). You'll want to obtain a logo, establish a presence on the internet, and possibly create a brochure. You might establish a full website or a simple landing page. Consider securing one or more domain names. You can start with your own name (e.g., www.paulabrand.com) and then add a business name. You will need to see if these names are available.

Just as professionals should network to advance their careers, you need to nurture and grow your network. Seek out business groups that can help you get established or grow your business (meetups, business associations, chambers of commerce, etc.).

Starting your own business can provide you career insurance by broadening your skill set and network, and providing income when you are in between jobs. It can offer an additional income stream when you are still working. Sometimes, it can even help you land a job.

It is possible to try to establish a business in parallel with a job search. In fact, one activity can complement the other if the business is related to the work you seek (e.g., a project manager who starts a project management consulting firm while also looking for a project manager position). In some cases, the two paths may conflict (e.g., you are a massage therapist trying to establish a massage business at the same time as trying to get hired by potential competitors). In this case, you might keep your entrepreneurial ambitions to yourself when interviewing. Ultimately, you need to decide at the beginning of the process what percentage of your time you want to devote to each career goal. Some of the necessary tasks will overlap and help you move forward with both goals, but others will focus plenty of tasks toward one end game.

Recommended reading

As an entrepreneur, I have found the following books to be helpful (in alphabetical order by author). They can be very useful when starting your business.

The E Myth Revisited by Michael E. Gerber: This book does make you think about the realities of starting your own business. I credit it for making me think about metrics from the beginning (tracking the number of inquiries, the number of clients, and any pertinent data about those clients). A wise colleague once told me to only track what I will use. You don't want to waste time tracking what you won't analyze and put to use. There are different versions of the E Myth for specific industries, but the original book will work for most businesses as a starting point.

This Is Marketing by Seth Godin: Marketing guru Seth Godin offers great insights on marketing concepts and gives illustrative examples to help you implement successful marketing strategies.

The Marketing Book by Jason McDonald: This book also emphasizes collecting and analyzing data to make business decisions, mainly in the realm of social media and advertising.

Book Yourself Solid by Michael Port: This book shares excellent advice on starting a service-based business. He explains some non-negotiable principles to live by (like dumping the clients you enjoy the least) and how to set up a sales process that builds upon itself.

Erin's story

As mentioned above, it's important to have a plan in place. It's also important to be flexible because you may have to make adaptations along the way. Let me share the example of Erin to illustrate some of the concepts in this chapter, along with some of the ideas in this book.

To provide some background, Erin held a part-time job during high school with a title company, which exposed her to the real estate industry. After graduation, she secured her first professional job with a local employer working as a title processor. Most of the work was related to residential transactions but also some commercial deals. Over the years, she mastered this job within different companies and was eventually recruited by a client of a former employer to be a real estate coordinator for McDonald's. She learned more about commercial real estate and excelled in this new environment. This was not a surprise, since the skills needed in both jobs were very similar. Erin has always been a highly organized and detail-oriented woman, and both roles required these strengths.

After many years in that role, she tried to develop within the company. She competed for and was selected to be a site acquisition manager. This involved some of the detailed work from before but also new responsibilities. She had to decide which sites the company should purchase, which added new responsibilities, such as assessing financial risks, and negotiating real estate contracts. In the end, this work made her uncomfortable. She didn't like negotiating, didn't feel she was good at it, and had little interest in developing this skill. The role wore on her as she simultaneously planned to start a family. Within a few years, she quit this job and had her first child. Up to this point, most of her career had not been planned out. She accepted opportunities that came along but rarely questioned her path.

Fast forward 10 years later. Now Erin had two young children and wanted to go back to work. She missed feeling productive in a work setting and knew the additional income could help save up for private schools. This time she had a plan. First, she took some time to reflect and decide if she wanted to go back into her old field or try something new. After assessing her V.I.N.E.S. and her situation, she decided to go back to title work. Erin made this conclusion with my consultation. We knew she could make the highest income in a role she had held before. She also knew that these types of jobs might consider part-time work, which she preferred. Finally, we assessed that this was the field where she had the most contacts, and we knew this would help her land a job faster.

She gave herself a timeline and began her search. Erin organized her time to devote part of each week to job search, while still balancing family responsibilities. Surprisingly, her first attempt paid off greatly. I say surprising because her method was unconventional. She is an avid user of Facebook and has many contacts on that platform. She asked me if it was okay to put something out there. I explained that Facebook was not the best method for job search, but it was worth trying since she had such a strong presence there. Erin revealed the content of her potential post, and I suggested that she change it from being very general to being very specific. Instead of sharing that she was back on the job market and asking if anyone knew of ANY jobs, I proposed that she share her specific goal of finding a part-time job doing title work in a real estate company.

She made the post and brushed up her resume. Within two months, she had many leads, which turned into five interviews at competing companies. She prepared for each encounter and received offers for all five positions. Ultimately, she picked the best offer based on location, hours, and company reputation.

But her story doesn't end there. After one year in this role, the COVID-19 pandemic began. Her office required her to work from home. With her children at home too because schools were initially suspended and then moved online, she found it too difficult to work from home while trying to meet her children's daily needs. Reluctantly, she submitted her resignation and left on good terms.

After her children were allowed to go back to school, she still had a desire to work but re-evaluated her situation and her V.I.N.E.S. Erin still wanted to work part time, but now she wanted to draw upon her love of gardening and flowers to create a new path. She applied for a job at a local florist but didn't even get a call back. Having no formal experience in this type of work proved to be a tough challenge.

Guess what she decided to do? She started her own business of selling flower arrangements. Having never done this before, she started with some experiments. She posted on Facebook to ask if anyone was interested in buying arrangements for Mother's Day and shared pictures of displays. At first, she didn't get much response, but after a friendly reminder post, suddenly she had plenty of requests for this occasion. Later, she tried a few more test runs and then started getting asked to provide flowers for weddings, First Communions, and celebrations of life. She is still feeling her way through this new phase. She has learned which flowers last longest and that she can use foliage from her own evergreens. She has grown flowers for her arrangements and found a few wholesale dealers to make the business more economical. It is a work in progress, and she is enjoying her new path.

As you can see from Erin's story, finding the right fit depends on where you are in your life. You are more likely to end up in the place you seek if you plan out a path and execute a plan. Sometimes, coincidence and serendipity will get you there, but that is much less common. You may hit roadblocks along the way. Sometimes, you have to employ different methods to achieve your goal. No matter what your next best step is, at each career crossroad, it is worthwhile to assess your V.I.N.E.S. and follow the A.S.T.E.R. Career Model to help you more forward.

SUMMARY

- In the execution phase, you have a few choices: get a job, develop in place, and/or start a business.

- No matter which route you choose, it's important to set realistic goals with deadlines, create a structure/routine, manage your time well, and network.

- Developing in place means staying in your current job while trying to change something about your situation to allow for growth.

- Starting a business might be a career option to consider. You should do thorough research before beginning.

- Consider thoughtfully answering key questions before jumping into entrepreneurship.

- If you do decide to create a business, map out the initial steps and seek out help as needed.

"No one will ever care as much about your job search or career as you."

PAULA BRAND, FOUNDER OF BRAND CAREER MANAGEMENT

CHAPTER ELEVEN

Job Search

If you are seeking employment, you need to buckle down and get serious. Looking for work is a job in itself. Create a routine that contains plenty of blocks of time for the activities integral to an intentional job search. Because this is hard work, you'll also want to build in rewards and breaks. I encourage you to pace yourself and have some fun in the process.

If you are not working, you probably have more time to do fun and out-of-the-ordinary things. It costs nothing to spend time with friends or walk around an interesting public place. Many community spaces like parks, museums, and exhibits are free. I often say that when you are unemployed, you have more time than money, and when you are employed, you have more money than time. While I want you to take your job search seriously, I also want you to do some things you've always wanted to do "if you only had time," because when you're not working, you often have more flexibility. Take advantage of it! I think 25 hours or so is plenty to give to your job search each week. Use some of your extra time to enjoy yourself. Doing so will help you maintain a positive attitude during your job search. Reconnect with former friends (a form of networking) or explore/renew a hobby.

I want to add a note here about setting boundaries with your time while you are in your job search. This point is especially true for women who often put others before themselves. When you are unemployed, people will ask you to do lots of favors that take up time—like watch their children, keep an eye on a neighbor, or give someone a ride. Just because you are not committed to a job, people inevitably think you have a lot of free time on your hands and don't realize that you might need to say no to these things because you are focused on your job search. Be true to yourself. Get some backbone, and say no to the requests that consume precious minutes you need to devote to finding the right job. Don't be guilted into thinking that your networking time isn't as important as helping watch someone's child just because it's not a job interview. Networking is the key to finding work! If you have any extra time on your schedule, you should use it on focused and strategic networking to land a job faster.

One last note about time management during your job search. It's okay if you take time off from your job search, if you can afford it, to tackle a really important matter. There may be some things you do want to help with or that you must handle that will take time and your situation gives you a chance to do them. Unique opportunities surfacing during your job search provide a chance for you to create balance. Unexpected things happen (your mom breaks her hip or you have a health issue), and when they do, it is a godsend you're not working because your availability allows you to take care of them. Life happens! Just be sure to get back to your job search as soon as you can. The longer you are unemployed, the harder it will be to get back into the workforce.

It takes discipline to be committed to a job search so it can be helpful to find an accountability partner to keep yourself on track. What I mean is someone else you will speak with regularly to share updates on your progress. Having another person who is also in job search mode is helpful because you will share an emotional tie to your situation. However, any person who is available, reliable, and interested in your success will do. Set regular intervals for checking in, and plan what you will cover when you speak (how many people you met with, how many interviews you landed, etc.). Please notice that I didn't say how many online applications you submitted because responding to posted openings is the worst way to find a job. This partner can also offer a sympathetic ear and help you brainstorm new ideas and strategies.

Since I mentioned the worst way to find a job, let me also mention that the best way to land a gig is through networking. Have you ever heard of the Hidden Job Market (HJM)? HJM refers to all of the jobs available that are not publicly advertised by an employer. It's the secret to job search success. The HJM is very large and accessible through human connections. Let me explain. Often someone knows about a potential opening. It could be her own job because she plans to leave soon but hasn't yet told her employer. It could be someone who knows someone else will be leaving soon. This could include someone who knows that a friend is moving out of the area for a job that a prospective employee must do in person or someone who knows of a colleague who plans to leave to start a family. It could even be a hiring manager who knows she must fire someone very soon. All these situations create opportunity in the HJM. How do you access the hidden job market? Through networking, of course, because none of these types of opportunities will be posted anywhere right away.

There is always a period of time when very few people know about a future opening. For example, once someone gives her notice, often initially only the supervisor knows about the vacancy. It is common for a manager to sit on this knowledge for a week or two because she is too busy to deal with it. A good manager will try to fill the position quickly, and therefore, she may ask around casually to see if anyone on the team knows of a good replacement. At this point, more than one person knows about the opportunity but still very few people know about it. After trying informal methods, the manager may have to use formal methods and may seek the help of HR.

The HR department often has standard procedures for posting a job that may include updating the job requirements. This often takes an additional week or two. It is not uncommon that four to five weeks will pass between the time an employee gives notice to the time that the job gets publicly posted. This time period also represents the HJM. While some companies must legally post all vacancies, most managers want to fill the position with the least amount of work. So, if you find a way to interact with a hiring manager when they are in the HJM phase of filling a position and you can communicate why you are a good fit, chances are you can secure an interview. As you can imagine, discovering an opening while it's still in the HJM phase will decrease your competition. Once the job is known to the world, your competition will increase exponentially.

Narrowing down your target companies

After going through the A-S-T parts of the A.S.T.E.R. Career Model, you know what you want to do. That's a start. Now you have to think more about where you want to do it. Consider travel time, the types of people you will be around, and the work environment. Take some time to reflect and record 10 employers where you think you might like to work.

1) _____

2) _____

3) _____

4) _____

5) _____

6) _____

7) _____

8) _____

9) _____

10) _____

Next, conduct research to test your assumptions that these really are great workplaces. Go online and evaluate the feel of their website. Do they seem to value the same things you might also value (for example, integrity, diversity, investing in their employees)? You can also visit websites like Glassdoor.com. This site provides anonymous employee reviews of employers. I wouldn't turn away from an employer because of one bad review, but I would look for trends. Also, seek out organizations that list and award employers for certain qualities. As an example, Seramount (formerly Workingmother) annually recognizes the 100 best companies for working mothers on its website at https://seramount.com/best-companies/, and the *Baltimore Business Journal* publishes an annual *Book of Lists*. These lists rank organizations and people who define industries in the Greater Washington, D.C. area. Surveys and research data can be expensive to purchase on your own, but most libraries offer free access to information collected about industries and employers.

If an organization seems like a good match, try to find someone who works there or even someone who knows someone who works there. Think broadly. Ask everyone you know. Ask friends, family, past colleagues, parents of your children's friends, and neighbors. You get the idea. Also, look the company up on LinkedIn (which will tell you if you have connections who work there). Ask to meet with these people to learn the inside scoop about the workplace culture and the types or volume of positions they seek to fill.

Go back to the company website to see if any names on the site look familiar. Go to the career page of the company website. Most large companies will have one. See what they look for in the talent they hire. Make a note of this information for future interviews.

Pick the top companies that resonated with you during your research. Use these to focus your efforts. It's a good idea to always have a list of 10 companies you are currently targeting. As you find out more about each one, you may want to remove one from the list. That is fine, but you need to replace it with a new potential company to explore. As you learn about a company, it may lead you to another company that does similar work. LinkedIn can be handy for this because when you are looking at job postings for one company, LinkedIn will point out comparable companies with similar jobs. Also, you can set up job alerts on LinkedIn to save time and effort.

I've mentioned Lauren's story in Chapters Two (Values) and Six (Skills). I'd like to share one more piece of her story related to targeting companies. In the end, this approach was the tipping point for her job search. She had begun the A.S.T.E.R. Career Model, which provided her with a very accurate sense of who she was and the type of company where she wanted to work. She had a lot of community contacts, and she was willing to network.

However, even after conducting informational interviews and extensive career exploration, she still struggled with committing to job titles as targets. It was becoming a barrier, so we moved our focus to targeting organizations. Since she knew she wanted to remain in her location and she knew she wanted a non-profit-type setting, I asked her to come up with a list of 10 local places where she thought she would feel proud to work.

Lauren did a great job vetting the list, and in doing so she landed her job. Through her extensive networking and diligent research, she found a non-profit with a leader she respected and work she believed in. This was a regional chapter of an internationally known organization helping people with disabilities. Ultimately, the CEO created a position of program developer for her.

How did this happen? Even though she could not 100% commit to the exact job title to target, she knew she wanted a job in the middle of an organization (without the stress of being on the front line or being at the top). She also knew the company would have to share her values (which narrowed down the field), and she started there. She gathered information about each potential employer, including their location and reputation. She also engaged in thorough self-reflection, was able to communicate her best skills, and show how they could be of value to an organization. She networked within her community and assessed her access to leaders. Where she didn't have a direct connection, she asked around to reveal tertiary connections. Lauren conscientiously followed through on every lead. It was her hard work that paid off but also her willingness to try a different approach to her job search.

The nuts and bolts of job search

Now that you have some job titles to target, along with top organizations to zero in on, you need to create marketing collateral ,including a resume. I know it's been well debated whether the resume is still necessary. I say, "Yes!". It's still a useful way for people to get to know you quickly, and it's something people will ask you for to try to help you land a job. It is often needed as part of the hiring process, and it forces you to get your thoughts together about what you've done and accomplished in your experience. It's not what's going to get you the job, but it should get you an interview, and it will definitely help you with networking.

Resumes

First off, I highly recommend having one master document that records everything from your work history. This could include the name of the employers, addresses, phone numbers, names of past supervisors, dates of employment, salary, and a list of your duties. This is way more information than most employers will ask for (unless it's the U.S. government), but it's good to have it all in one place for when you might need to access it. You will not share this document with others, so it doesn't have to look beautiful. It's for your reference purposes and can save you lots of time down the road. It's very helpful when completing applications, but you can also use it as a starting point when you need to create a resume. You will use this master document to create targeted resumes for specific opportunities. Over time, you may have shorter versions of your resume to work off of for similar types of jobs. This document will take time to develop, but it's worth the investment.

When you are ready to create a specific resume for a specific job target, you must decide on a style. There are different varieties of resumes, but they mainly fall into two styles: job-based or skill-based. A job-based resume is more commonly known as the chronological resume, and the bulk of its content will be a listing of your past jobs, in reverse-chronological order. Under each employment experience, you will list bullet points that share accomplishments that are quantified as much as possible.

175

This style is best if you are staying in the same role/field/industry, and you don't have any major gaps in your employment history.

Skill-based resumes, an alternative, go by different names, but the most common are functional, combination, or hybrid. The bulk of content on this style of resume will be sharing your key skills related to the job target (and it may not be obvious when or where you gained those skills). The most effective skill-based resumes share a brief work history somewhere on the document, but it's purposefully not the main focus. This allows employers to account for gaps in employment and see older titles that may be relevant while the focus remains on your skillset. **This style is best if you are changing careers, if you have large gaps in your work history, or if something you did a long time ago is what you are now targeting.**

To see examples of each resume style, go to the bonus page for this book found at purple-parachute.com/bonus. Below are some relevant tips.

Your resume is a marketing document, not a biographical history of your entire work experience. You want to keep it to about two pages, three at most, because the longer it is, the less likely others will read all of it.

In terms of past jobs, you don't need to include details beyond title, employer, and dates of employment, unless it serves a purpose (or if it's required, as in a U.S. federal application). Some jobs will not be present for various reasons (they are not relevant to the target, they were short-lived positions, they are too old, etc.). You must keep the document focused! Everything on it should make the case for your candidacy. You should remove all other information.

Let me share an example related to geography. If you live in Washington, D.C., all of your jobs have been in the D.C. area, and you are applying for a job in D.C., you might want to include the location of each employer, along with your city of residence. This will show that you are local, which implies that you have an established network and won't need relocation. However, if you have the same circumstances but you are trying to get a job in Denver, CO, you might purposefully leave off the cities where you've worked because it might imply that your network is not in Denver but only in Washington, D.C. In that case, if you have a local connection to Denver (maybe you grew up there), you could mention this fact in your cover letter.

To take it a step further, let's consider your contact information. Keeping your current location off the top of your resume may help avoid the initial screener ruling you out right away by your location alone. If a human is reading your resume, anything but a local address is an easy reason to put you in the "no" pile. This is because local candidates have an advantage. Hiring locals is seen as a less risky move because they don't have to uproot their lives, and they are more affordable since there's no need to pay for them to relocate.

In Applicant Tracking Systems or ATS (these are software programs that allow employers to accept and store applicant data), recruiters can narrow down search results by including a zip code or city name as a search term. If possible, use a local address (of a friend/family member or buy a P.O. box) to help you avoid getting screened out due to location. Or consider leaving off your current location altogether.

After your contact information, use an introductory paragraph (or bulleted sentences) before jumping into the rest of the resume. You can call it many things: career profile, career summary, or summary of qualifications. It's a compelling three- to four-sentence summary of your background. Though most of this section won't need to change, you can modify this section for each resume as it relates to the job target. Why do you need this section? Because if you don't provide it, you force the person to read the entire document to see if you are a good fit. Hiring professionals are busy and don't have this much time. They might receive hundreds of resumes for one job, so you need to make it easy to see your qualifications up front. If you don't, you'll go in the "no" or "maybe read later" pile.

After your contact information and career summary, it's usually best to begin the bulk of your job-based or skill-based content (depending on which style you chose). After that, other sections you might include are education, certifications, leadership/volunteer work, organizations you belong to, awards received, languages, and technology skills.

In terms of writing style for the descriptions under each employment experience or skill, you don't want your sentences to sound like a job description because you'll put the reader to sleep. You can use a formal job description as a starting point, but you must edit the words by adding how you actually fulfilled the role and the impact you made.

Each sentence must start with an action verb (never start with a pronoun or "responsible for"). For example, instead of "I compiled data daily for weekly reports," you would say, "Compiled daily data for weekly reports." Also, be sure to give some description and not just a list of topical areas. I have seen some resumes that look like this:

Accountant	ABC Company	Dates worked

- Reconciled
- Internal auditor
- Handled inquiries
- Payroll

This is a starting point, but you need to give more description about these tasks. Turn them into sentences, starting with an action verb and quantify them. Maybe share how many people are on the payroll. How large an account have you reconciled? How often do you audit the books? What types of inquiries do you handle? How often and how fast do you solve the questions?

I can't emphasize this enough: All statements and bulleted sentences sharing your past jobs or skills need to be quantified as much as possible! Quantified statements always make more of an impact than a list of duties. With so many words on the paper, the human eye tends to jump to numbers. Digits and percentages stand out on a resume. I admit that some jobs are easier to quantify than others, but with enough effort, anyone can quantify parts of their job. Jobs in sales or finance naturally lend themselves to quantification. The number of sales made, the size of budgets, and amounts of time and money saved are numerically stated. With administrative jobs, think about how often you do something (daily, weekly, monthly, quarterly, or annually), or how much time you have saved by streamlining a process. In any job, how do you measure your progress? For some, it will be the number of clients/patients/patrons/customers assisted; for others, it might be the number of hits to a website; and others, it might be the number of customer disputes resolved (along with how fast and how often).

Give context and use stats to your advantage. If your number is not impressive, you don't have to include it, but when numbers are big, share them. For example, if you manage one or two people, I would state: "Managed staff, including hiring, training, developing, disciplining, and firing." However, if you manage 20 or more people, you should state the number in that sentence. And always go for the highest number you can claim. If you normally manage 20 people but at times it was only 10, you can still state, "Managed up to 20 staff at one time." I purposefully used the number, and so should you. Numbers draw attention on a resume, so write out the number if you want the employer to notice it.

Here is an example of how adding numbers can give context and depth to your sentences. Which person would you hire as a receptionist: someone who lists "Answered phone calls" or someone who writes, "Answered and directed incoming phone calls (up to 200 daily on a 10-line phone system)?"

Here's another tip for quantifying: Use statistics to your advantage. Which sentence sounds better: "Increased trainee attendance from one to two people", or "Increased trainee attendance by 100%?" This is a simple example, but it makes my point.

Here are some final resume tips for success:

- Never use smaller than 10-point font (any smaller may be hard to read).

- Use common fonts. The more unusual the font, the less likely the reviewer's computer will be able to read your document. They will not write you back to ask for it in a different font—they will just move on to the next resume.

- Refrain from jargon and abbreviations only known in your company or industry. The person reading your resume, such as the initial screener, may not know them.

- Spell check will catch most typos but not always. Double check your work, and have someone else conduct a final proofreading. After you've looked at it so many times, you will not see simple typos.

- Know your audience and analyze the job posting before targeting your resume. Your resume must speak to the reader.

- Consistency is critical in resumes. Use periods or none. Either is fine, but you can't end some sentences with periods and not others.

- If one section heading is in bold and capitalized, all of them should be.

- Although one inch is the formal amount of space for margins, you can get away with as small as half an inch.

Finally, don't put the most compelling qualifications at the end. For example, if you speak French and English and that is a job requirement, you might put something that says that to the reader up front—maybe by using the word bilingual to describe yourself in the career summary (and later listing which languages) or finding a way to share near the top of the document that you are fully fluent in English and French. If you only list your language skills at the bottom of page two, they may be missed.

Recommended reading

Two resume experts I highly respect for their resume savvy are Wendy Enelow and Louise Kursmark. They have two resume books you might find helpful:

Modernize Your Resume: Get Noticed ... Get Hired (2nd Edition) in paperback only

The Best Keywords for Resumes, Letters, and Interviews: Powerful Words and Phrases for Landing Great Jobs! in paperback and on Kindle

Cover letters

You're not alone if you feel this is the hardest part of applying for a job. Many people struggle with cover letters. While it is a necessary formality for most job submissions, in reality, not every employer will read every cover letter. For any professional level job submission, the employer will expect a cover letter. However, not all jobs (such as entry level or in the trades) require it. That said, it will never hurt you unless it's poorly written, has lots of typos, or is presented badly (think coffee stain on white paper).

I would focus more on your resume development and less time grappling over every word on your cover letter. If you have networked well, your cover letter will matter even less. To ease the amount of work for you (and the reviewer), try your best to keep it to one page.

For any job that involves writing or administration, the cover letter becomes more important because it's a sample of your future work. If your format, grammar, and writing style are weak, the reader may assume that is the general quality of your work and potentially how you would prepare something on behalf of the employer.

I suggest using a basic formula for your cover letters for most jobs. The more unusual or creative the job, the more leeway you have in making an "out of the box" presentation. For "standard" jobs, I suggest going with the status quo (below).

First paragraph: State why you are writing and applying for this position. If possible, mention the job posting details (title or number), and if you have a referral from someone, state this up front. You can add details as to why you are interested in the job/company. You can also share what you know about the company and how you can meet their needs.

Make it employer-focused, not you-focused. For example, don't state that you really want this job because you're moving to Denver and need a job there. The employer doesn't care about your wants and needs. They care about how well you fit the position requirements.

Second paragraph: Explain how your background and experience fit the job requirements. Make this as simple for the reader as possible. If you match the job well, making a side-by-side comparison of the requirements and your experience can be very effective. You can do this by creating a table in Word and then hide the lines. If you are going for a paragraph format, share some sentences about your past experiences that give proof you can perform the job duties with excellence.

Third paragraph: Close the letter by offering thanks to the reader ("Thank you for your consideration"). You may mention that you plan to follow up to ensure it was received (this gives you an excuse to make contact in the future). If you say that, make sure you actually do it (which will build trust right away that you are a woman of your word). Always share contact information at the top of the document or in the closing paragraph (in case your letter and resume are separated).

One last point, always try to address your letter to a specific person and avoid addressing it to "Sir/Madam." I suggest giving yourself 20 minutes to see if you can find a name. At the very least, address it to the "Hiring Manager." Here are some tips on trying to find the right name.

Call the main number and ask for the name of the person reviewing applications for that job. Before COVID-19, it could be as simple as that. Now it's harder to get a human receptionist.

If it's a blind ad but they gave a phone or fax number, google that data to see if you can find the company name or website. There are resources online that allow you to search for a person or entity by providing a phone number. They are generally called "reverse phone" directories. Many are free, but some do charge so be sure to watch for unreasonable costs.

If you do get a name and you know the domain name of the company, try to guess the person's email. For example, if the company's domain name is abx.com and you can see from the website that most emails are the person's first initial followed by their last name, you could guess that the right email might be pbrand@abx.com. It's worth a shot!

It can be helpful to send a copy directly to the hiring manager. This person is rarely the same person who is looking through the first pile of resumes. To be transparent, you can do this in addition to sending one to HR and you can cc both parties. You don't want to get HR mad at you for trying to bypass them. At the same time, the hiring manager often knows best what they want, and if you can access and pitch that person in a compelling way, sometimes you can get them to arrange an interview right away (especially if they are on a tight time frame).

If the posting asks for your salary history or salary requirements, I suggest that you avoid giving them this information because giving your salary history at this point puts you at a great disadvantage for later negotiations. Also, if you give your specific salary requirements, you may knock yourself out of the running. Of course, you do take a slight risk that a strict reviewer will put you in the "no" pile because you didn't answer the question, but I have yet to meet a hiring manager who said that they would not consider a great resume because of this one omission on a cover letter. To cover your bases, you can address the request by stating, "My salary requirements are negotiable based on the full compensation package."

I made this mistake once. I gave my salary requirement in a cover letter to a local college (and I aimed a little high because I was already employed). I hadn't heard anything, so I later followed up and got the hiring manager on the phone (using the suggestions mentioned above). We hit it off, and she asked me to send her my resume. She was so convinced I was a good candidate that she said she would look into the reason my resume was not in the pile of candidates sent to her by HR.

In a second conversation with the hiring manager, I learned that HR put me in the "no" pile because my stated requirement was $50,000 but the position salary the company offered was firmly set at $45,000. However, she also explained that this employer had amazing benefits, one of which was free classes. I said that all sounded good to me. I continued through the process and received employment. Sharing my requirement hurt me, and if I had not followed up, I would have never gotten that job.

INTERVIEWING

If you've secured an interview, hooray for you! Now you want to take it seriously and prepare as much as possible to give your best performance. I use the word performance on purpose. Just like an actor, you have to work on your presentation and know your lines to land the job offer or move yourself to the next level of competition.

Where are you going?

For an in-person interview, when invited to the interview, be sure to ask for an address and if there's anything you should know about arriving: Is there a visitor entrance or a specific building? Will you need to show an ID? Is parking available? etc. Some employers have a huge campus, like colleges. Some have multiple locations, and you want to make sure you're going to the right one. The National Institutes of Health main campus is so big that there is a shuttle bus you must use to get around, and it can take an hour to get your visitor ID badge. It's important to get to the right place, so use technology to look up the address and figure out the best way to get there. In a small town, logistics can be simple, but in a big city they can take more planning, especially if you are going to take a taxi or use public transportation. If you are able, I highly recommend doing a dry run in the week before to test out your planned path. Make sure you practice at a similar time of day using the same path you will take on the actual day of your interview. Knowing exactly how to get there and what you might encounter should ease some of your nerves.

If your interview is virtual, which has become the norm thanks to COVID-19, you need to review a new set of considerations. Most importantly, plan to have your virtual interview in a quiet and private space. Consider the lighting. Ensure that any incoming light is facing you. If it's behind you, shadows will fall on your face, making it hard for the interviewer to see your facial expressions. Make sure to clean up the area behind you. A messy environment with stacks of folders and empty coffee mugs will not make a good first impression.

Ahead of the meeting, try to test things out. If the employer is using recruiting software like HireVue, you may not be able to simulate the exact scenario. However, you can still use a free platform like Zoom to mimic things as best you can. During the interview, maintain eye contact by looking at the camera (not the person on your screen). This takes some practice because our eye naturally goes to the person we see on the screen, but if you do that, you will not be making eye contact. It can help to place a picture of a loved one right next to the camera to remind you to look there.

Who will you be meeting?

It's very helpful to know how many people will be interviewing you. A one-to-one encounter can have a more informal feel than a five-member interview panel, whether virtual or in-person. No matter the situation, it's always a good idea to research the people/panel ahead of time.

One-to-one interviews: Do your best to build rapport right away. Since it is only one person, you really should try to find out something about the person before the meeting. Going to their LinkedIn profile can assist in this area. A simple Google search will frequently offer anecdotal information, like interests, affiliations, and causes.

Panel interviews: When you are interviewing with a panel (usually three to five people), the most important thing to do is treat each person with the same respect. This means if you shake one hand, shake all hands, and look each person in the eye. The best way to do this is to focus about 80% of your eye contact with the person who asked the question. Spend the rest of your time gliding your eyes from one person to another, so you make every person there feel connected to each answer.

Do your research

Research as much as you can about the position, the company, and the industry. It's very common to hear, "What do you know about our company?" If you can't answer this question, you're not going to get the job. A colleague once complained to my brother how hard it was to fill a position. He had interviewed eight people for a position that paid about $80,000/a year with a publicly traded company and not one of them had a decent answer to that question. Because of that, he decided to avoid all of them and restart the recruitment process from scratch.

It's hard to believe with so much information on the internet that someone would go into an interview without this knowledge. You don't have to know every single fact about the company, but you should know some answers to the following questions: What is their mission statement (if they have one)? What do they offer? Who are their customers? Who is the current leader? How long has that person been leading the company? When was the company started? What is the size of the company (the number of employees, customers, or locations should give you a good idea)? Who are their biggest competitors? How have they performed in recent years? If it's a public entity, this information should be very easy to find. If it's a private company, you'll need to rely more on networking and word of mouth. If it's a non-profit organization, their annual IRS Form 990 can be accessed publicly. They contain critical financial information, including the salaries of the five highest paid employees. This can be useful data for future salary negotiations.

If the company has a website and a page dedicated to careers, see what they say on that page. It might share core values they seek in employees. If it does, be sure to mention in your interview how your values align with those of the employer. If they mentioned unique and specific words, try to work those into your answers. As an example, I was doing a mock interview with a client and I had done my own research on the company to prepare. The company had a career page and mentioned five characteristics they look for in their employees. One trait was being scrappy, and they defined it as being resourceful and determined to get things done. During the mock interview I asked the candidate, "Would you say you're a scrappy person?" I could tell from her answer she did not check out the company website because she had to ask me what I meant by that term. Her answer was okay considering she was obviously surprised by my question, but it was a wasted opportunity. During our debrief, I explained why I asked her that question. We also discussed how a little more preparation (going to the company career webpage before the interview) could have given her a great opportunity to share how scrappy she can be. She could have mentioned it in her answer to "Tell me about yourself." If asked, "What is your greatest strength?" she could have prepared an answer that gave a concrete example of a time when she was successfully scrappy.

The C-A-R method

There is a great technique called the C-A-R interview method, which stands for challenge, action, results. You may have also heard it as S-T-A-R, P-A-R, or S-A-R. These catchy acronyms express a tried-and-true method for answering many interview questions. It works best for behavioral questions but might apply to other questions such as, "What is your greatest strength?" The idea is to give a concrete example that backs up your claim.

The C-A-R method works for two reasons. First, it gives a structure for your answer, which can help keep you focused and on point. Too many people blow job interviews by rambling on. Second, it makes the story easy for the listener to follow. They hear the story in the C-A-R format with a beginning, middle, and end, so it's clearly understood.

For example, if someone asks you, "What is your greatest strength?" you cannot just reply, "I'm really great at staying calm under pressure! You wouldn't believe it" and leave it at that. You must illustrate your point to them, and the best way to do that is by telling a C-A-R story. People remember stories!

So, here's what you would want to add to the previous statement: "Let me share an example of how calm I can be under pressure based on my experience with a former client."

C (Challenge): "A few years ago, I worked for an international development organization stationed in Asia during monsoon season. I was taking a group of high-level officials to a remote island by helicopter for a tour. Unfortunately, during our time there, we were warned to leave ASAP due to an unexpected severe storm."

A (Action): "Understanding the gravity of the situation, I promptly gathered the group, who were in varied parts of the island, in a short amount of time. One of the ministers was being difficult and wanting to stay longer. He was using his powerful position to challenge me in front of the others and trying to buy more time on the island. I had to use expert diplomacy and tact to persuade him (and the others) that this warning was very serious and that we all needed to go right away. It was a challenge, but I finally got him to comply and express the message to others."

R (Result): "We took off minutes before the storm hit. As we rose into the sky, we could see the approaching darkness. We landed safely on the mainland, but it did prove to be a very severe monsoon. The minister and pilot later thanked me for being calm and persistent in the face of danger. The storm was so devastating, and we would have been stranded on that island for days if we had stayed a minute longer."

Here are some additional tips for using the C-A-R method

When describing the challenge, be sure to be brief. This should not be the bulk of the story, but it is necessary for context. If you were under a tight time frame or this was a challenging task for some reason, this could be the place to mention it.

If you have to put someone down (i.e., "Because my boss messed up, I was stuck doing..."), use a different story or remove that part of it. You could start with, "Due to some unforeseen circumstances, I found myself needing to jump into a new situation." This leaves out bad-mouthing your boss while still expressing the challenge of the situation.

When explaining actions, it's important to be clear what role you played if it was part of a team effort. Avoid saying "we did..." too much. If you state everything as "we," it's hard for the listener to know what exactly you did. Instead, you can say, "Our team was assigned tasks with XYZ, and my role was to lead the team and take care of ABC. I did this by..." Also, be sure to point out times when you initiated the implemented idea. Employers love to see initiative. If you don't mention it, they may assume you were carrying out someone else's great idea.

When sharing results, you can use quantitative and qualitative information. If you have statistics, those are often the most compelling results to share. Here are some examples of using data for your results: You can say that attendee evaluations of the conference suggested that 95% of those who attended the event would recommend it to a colleague, or your streamlining efforts reduced a turnaround time from three days to one.

Sometimes, hard data is not available or the type of work doesn't lend itself to quantitative data. In these cases, you can mention more qualitative results. These could include observations by colleagues, recognition in a performance review, or receiving an award. Emulation and knowledge sharing can be more examples of proof. For example, maybe your idea was adopted by others as a best practice, or you've been asked to share your findings with others in a white paper or at a conference.

Interview questions to expect

Below are common interview questions that many of my clients have trouble answering. With each question, I give some tips for answering it.

When asked... *"Tell me about yourself?"* This is not the time to share personal information, such as your marital status, and you should not bring up your children. These facts have nothing to do with how well you can do the job, and the employer may hold them against you. You can share personal information if it has professional implications. For example, if you run marathons, you could mention this because it also implies that you are disciplined and healthy, and can set goals (all things employers value in an employee).

However, you mainly want to focus on your career from a big-picture view. You can say things like, "In all of my roles, I've always been the go-to person for XYZ" or "All of my former bosses have recognized me for my consistent ability to deliver projects on time." You can also mention some of your strengths and key aspects of past roles as they relate to the job.

What you do not want to do is walk them through your resume job by job, duty by duty. There is not enough time for that, and you'll likely bore them to tears. Instead of saying, "I started out my career at X company and then I moved on to..." try saying something like, "I started out in the private sector in IT and later translated that background into a position running a non-profit helping others learn new technology." An ideal answer will be about three minutes. This is a decent amount of time to make your points but not enough for your life story.

When asked... *"What is your greatest strength?"* Even though the question asks for only one, I suggest having two strengths ready to share. Each should have its own C-A-R- story to back it up. Both should remain tied to strengths needed for the job at hand. If they only ask for one, don't make the common mistake of listing a handful of strengths without a C-A-R story.

Usually, you are only asked for one strength, but on occasion they may ask for several. If they do, you can list a few but stick to a C-A-R story to illustrate one in detail. There won't be enough time for multiple C-A-R stories. If you only use one strength for this question, you can probably work the other one into a different answer.

When asked... *"What is a weakness?"* First of all, you can't say you don't have any because we all have at least one. If you say that, it gives away your biggest weakness—lack of self-awareness. You must provide an answer and it's best if you are strategic about it. Let me share my "weakness formula" for answering this question.

First, create a list of weaknesses for you as a person (not just from a worker perspective). Save this list for any future interview. It may sound silly, but I have a file of weaknesses listing them. When I think of a new one, I add it to the list. Some of my biggest weaknesses are not being super creative, not being great with numbers, and not functioning well in a chaotic environment. What are some of yours? Write them down.

Next, select a weakness from your list that is NOT critical to the job you seek. You can't interview for an accounting position and admit that you are weak with numbers. Then, share some information that describes your awareness of the weakness and how you have been working to overcome it. What mental compensation techniques have you created for yourself? For example, if impatience is a weakness, you could explain that you make a point to wait at least 48 hours before following up with a co-worker. If public speaking is a weakness, you could share that you joined Toastmasters and you have started forcing yourself to contribute an idea in large group meetings.

Finally, share observations from others to prove that you are making progress. You could say that your colleagues have noticed and complimented you on sharing more of your ideas in public. You could mention that you have completed a Toastmasters certification or won a Toastmasters speech contest. Maybe your boss documented a comment from your last performance review stating a "noticeable improvement of contributing more in team meetings" and you can share this development.

One last piece of advice on handling this question that comes from my father (a former executive recruiter): Don't be afraid of silence. My dad used to ask the weakness question and purposefully pause after the answer was given. He said more times than not, the interviewee would feel uncomfortable in the silence so they would offer up another weakness and another, until they had talked themselves out of the job. As he advised with any question in an interview, answer the question, then smile and wait patiently for the next question.

When asked... *"What do you know about our company?"* This question is a measure of your motivation and is usually asked to see what research you have done on the company/division/department. If you can't answer this, odds are you will not get an offer for the job. If you did not take the time to prepare for this question, they might presume that you are not excited enough about the possibility of working there. They are not expecting perfection because you don't work there yet, but they expect a decent attempt to summarize what they are all about.

Go to their website and gather some basic facts: Is it a public entity, non-profit, or private company? What are their main lines of business/services? Who are their biggest competitors? Where are their locations? What year did they begin? What is the name of the current leader? These facts should be enough for you to give a basic summary of the company. If possible, it's good to talk with someone who works there (or worked there recently) to see if the words on the website match the reality within the company.

If they share the company values on the website or what they value in employees on their careers page, be sure to mention how these are aligned with your values to show how you could fit into their workplace culture. Never bring up bad news, like the fact that they didn't hit earning predictions last quarter.

Questions you can ask the interviewer(s)

At the end, most interviewer(s) will ask if you have any questions. Saying no is unacceptable and will give the impression that you are not interested in the job. I suggest that you prepare a few questions ahead of time and write them on a pad of paper. This avoids wasting mental energy trying to remember your questions for the end throughout the interview. The pad could be brought to an in-person interview or be at your fingertips during a virtual interview.

Questions you can ask at the end of the interview

"If I were hired for this position, what are the top challenges that I would need to address in the first 30 days?" You can adapt to 60 or 90 days if that is more appropriate.

It's okay to show some confidence by phrasing the question like this: "If the person hired is a great success, what would they have accomplished in the first year?" This might be better if you feel uncomfortable suggesting you would be hired.

"Who will supervise the work and where will the work be performed?" This is a basic question, but it works for almost any job.

If something naturally piques your curiosity during the interview, it's appropriate to inquire about it at the end.

If you absolutely can't think of any question, at least say that you had some questions prepared but they've all been answered during the interview.

Questions interviewees should not ask

Never ask anything too nosy, such as, "I read that there is some disagreement among the leadership on the next direction for your company. Is that true?"

Never ask anything that puts the interviewer(s) on the defense, such as, "I hear your turnover is very high. What do you think is causing that?"

Never ask anything that could have been easily discovered on the company website. It will make you look unprepared and lazy.

Think about the type of information that would be better to ask through an informal setting like a networking event. For example, you may want to know why the position is open, but that could be a touchy topic if it's because the last person died or was fired for unethical behavior. If you know someone at the company, ask that person these types of questions outside of the interview.

Interview musts

You must not be late. I know of one person who missed the interview due to a car breakdown and still got the job, but this is very rare. I knew an HR person who would not even meet with you if you were late. Arriving 10 to 15 minutes ahead of time is perfect for in-person interviews. It allows you enough time to fill out some brief paperwork, go to the bathroom to check yourself, and be less rushed.

For virtual interviews, start to get ready about 30 minutes before. Place water beside you, go to the bathroom, and make sure you have the instructions available. Try to join the meeting a few minutes early. Allow time to login to any system and don't be surprised if the interviewer is already there quietly waiting. Plan to make small talk while waiting for others to join the meeting. Or if things seem chaotic, wait patiently to show that you can be graceful.

SUMMARY

- For a job search, after narrowing down your job targets, explore target companies and prepare as necessary. This includes creating targeted resumes and preparing wholeheartedly for each interview.

- Consider the different styles of resumes. Figure out which will be the best presentation for your situation overall and tailor each resume to each job you want.

- Use the C-A-R (Challenge, Action, Results) method to prepare compelling stories for your interview.

- Prepare for common questions that you will be asked and that you should ask in an interview.

"Stepping onto a brand new path is difficult, but not more difficult than remaining in a situation which is not nurturing to the whole woman."

MAYA ANGELOU

CHAPTER TWELVE

Repeat The Process

You will likely go through the A.S.T.E.R. Career Model process many times during your career. Going through multiple career transitions in your life has become the new normal. In fact, the U.S. Department of Labor suggests that most people will have multiple careers (not just jobs) in their lifetime. You might switch jobs to start a new career path or because the company laid you off. You might have to make job changes because of life circumstances (marriage, relocation, illness, death, divorce, having a child, etc.). All of these events will create transitions in your life that you must process.

Dramatic life changes commonly cause one to rethink the purpose of work and its role in one's life. I've seen many situations when a woman decides to change her career after the loss of her remaining parent. I've also seen many times when a divorce suddenly thrusts a woman back into the workforce. These situations may involve stressful decisions, yet they also provide a newfound freedom to take risks.

Women in particular experience more career transition than men, mainly because of their ability to bear children and the likelihood they are the primary caregivers in their family (for children and elders). Taking a break from the workplace, no matter how big or small, creates transition. No matter the reason for the shift, there are things to consider that affect any type of change. Let's look to two experts on this topic for some guidance.

Well-respected career counselor Nancy Schlossberg created a theory on transitions, which was a culmination of insights after going through her own transitions. The Schlossberg Transition Theory focuses on the 4 S's that need assessment and addressing when someone is going through a transition: situation, self, support, and strategies. This framework is geared towards career professionals, but any layperson can understand the practical nature of her theory.

First, look at the situation. Are there many changes happening at once? Was this a forced choice? How do you feel about the circumstances? Obviously, with multiple changes at once, expect higher stress and the need for more support. Forced changes are always tougher than those we choose.

Second, look at your self. Have you faced a similar situation in the past? If so, how did you overcome it? What is your general coping mechanism? Is it healthy and productive? What can you do to help yourself during this time of transition? At the very least, practice self-compassion, and take care of your health by getting plenty of sleep, healthy foods, and exercise.

Third, assess your support system. What support do you need right now? Do you have others to lean on? Who will you ask and when? Do you need to seek mental health services? Do you need to hire assistance for some tasks? Be honest with yourself and don't let your pride prevent you from asking for help. Reach out to your supportive communities.

Fourth, implement strategies. Sometimes, you need to reframe the situation. Instead of feeling pushed out of a job you don't fit well, look at it as an opportunity to start a new role that you can enjoy. How will you manage the emotions of what you're going through? Where can you seek assistance? What is in your control? What isn't?

William Bridges is another guru of transition, and he has two very important concepts to share about transition:

1. **Change is what happens (the event); transition is how we experience it (with emotion and logic).** Whether we chose the change or not shapes our response. Usually, if we have chosen the change, we will adjust to it easily. Either way, you must work through the transition to come out on the other side. Ignoring your feelings and thoughts to avoid dealing with the transition is a wasted opportunity. Closing your eyes to the emotions of transition won't make them go away. Sooner or later, you will have to face the consequences of your new reality.

2. **There is a cycle of transition: the ending of something, the beginning of something new, and a neutral zone in between.** You must honor

each phase to move through the transition successfully. Ultimately, you must let go of the old to move into the neutral zone. Most people want to spend the shortest time in the neutral zone, but this is an essential phase that can't be rushed. It's also where you grow as a person. It takes time, but eventually you are ready to start a new beginning.

Change is usually happening faster than we like. Each time you come to a career crossroads or a life transition that affects your career, you may get stuck. To work through this, go through the A.S.T.E.R. Career Model, discover where you are in the cycle, and take the steps that will push you forward.

If change is happening more slowly than you would like, periodically ask yourself these questions:

Am I getting bored with the skills I constantly use in this job?

Am I fulfilled in my work role? If not, what is missing?

Are there more career experiences I would like to have in the future? What are they?

Am I contributing to a mission I believe in? Am I being recognized for my contribution?

Do I have purpose in my work?

Always have an idea of something you might want to do in the next few years for your career management. Set goals for yourself. These can be concretely set in an action plan or be more fluid in a mind map to get a holistic perspective on your career goals. Think about the future in the way that is most beneficial for your style of reflecting, but make time to envision your future. As the old saying goes, "If you don't set a destination, how will you know when you have arrived?"

Some things to consider when dreaming about your professional future and working on your career management:

What is my professional reputation? Am I happy with it? If not, what can I do to change it?

Do I need to update my personal/professional brand after making a career change?

Is my LinkedIn profile up-to-date?

Assuming I like to collaborate with others, with what types of people do I enjoy working?

Is there another way to generate income (as an entrepreneur, as a side gig, as a contractor)? Will it draw upon current skills or do I need to develop new skills to make this a reality?

Where do I want to be located for my work or do I want to work remotely?

Do I have a strong network of people I can rely on for career decisions and support? If not, what am I going to do to change that?

Am I satisfied with my job/career? If so, what's going well? If not, what is not going well?

What can I learn from any failures in my career?

Career resilience

Career resilience is your ability to manage through tough times, recover, and come back a little stronger. It is a necessity for effective career management, especially in our world of constant change. It could be considered a mindset or a skill. The good news is that you can develop resilience. The most important aspect of career resilence is growing and learning. If you hit a setback in your career, take time to reflect upon it. Was there anything in your control that you could have done to change the outcome? Did a challenge present itself that helped you gain a new skill or insight? Was there a lesson learned to possibly prevent a repeat of this scenario?

Let me point to a personal example and share the roughest patch of my career. After taking a brief break from the workforce, I landed a job with a former employer in workforce development. It was in the same role as before but under a new boss. I received a warning about my potentially new supervisor. Rumor had it that she was a bully and bad manager and didn't care about the program. I wanted to give the job a chance, so I took it anyway, and within one month, I quit with no next job lined up. This was something I never recommend and had never done before, but the workplace environment was untenable. I had to leave to save my sanity and integrity.

Shortly after this, I landed what I thought was my dream job in a career center at a local college. Unfortunately, after only three months, I was essentially fired for the first and only time in my career. I was devastated about losing this job, and it was humiliating to be escorted from the building when I had done nothing wrong.

After these two incidents in a short period of time, I lost my confidence and started to wonder what was wrong with me. I investigated to try to find out more about what happened. I discovered that the woman who fired me had a questionable record of behavior, and the college let some questionable managers run their departments with little accountability. Incidentally, around this time, the college held a town hall explaining the suddenly dire situation of the college's finances.

To get past this time, I had to draw upon close friends and colleagues. They helped me with job leads, confidence building, and assurances that I had what it takes. I followed my own advice and reviewed past accomplishments to remember the awesome work I had done before this time period. And, of course, I implemented the A.S.T.E.R. Career Model to confirm that I wanted to stay on this career path. All of these steps helped me survive and then thrive again. Ironically, I returned to the same employer in workforce development but this time in a new program and a different boss.

In reflecting on the situations and understanding my role in them, I came to a few conclusions. First, if I am ever warned by multiple and reasonable sources about a potentially bad boss, don't take the job. Another lesson was that I needed to do the same amount of due diligence for all jobs, no matter how well I know the organization. In addition, I learned that it's good to check the financial status of your future organization. Though it was never officially confirmed, I believe budgetary reasons were behind my firing. I now knew that the college was facing extreme financial difficulties, and it is a common practice let go of the most recently hired employee. Most importantly, I learned to trust my instincts because in retrospect, I could see signs that I ignored. Overall, I now see the positives of these experiences. They taught me mistakes I have not repeated. It was invaluable as a career professional to have personally gone through these tough times because they increased the empathy I have for my clients and made me a better advisor.

Below are some ways to increase your career resilience:

1. **Stay healthy:** We'll start with the basics. Get a good night's sleep. If you're not able to, figure out why and take action to change. Keep your body moving, even if it's just walking for 30 minutes a few times a week. Get out in nature and enjoy the outdoors. Eat nutritious foods. Seek out support when needed. Find healthy ways to relieve stress, such as meditation. These apps offer meditation guidance with free and paid subscriptions: Headspace, https://www.headspace.com/; Calm, https://www.calm.com/; and Insight Timer, https://insighttimer.com/. Each site has a different feel, so try them out first to see which is the best fit for you.

2. **Continue learning:** Because of the rapid pace of change in the world today, you must be willing to learn new skills, particularly when it comes to keeping up with tech-driven changes that affect your field. I don't subscribe to the idea that AI will replace all of our jobs in a gloom and doom scenario, but I do accept that automated tasks and processes are likely to become more a machine function than a human job (for example, cashiers in retail settings). In some cases, this will require people to be able to program and run the machines, which will create new jobs. However, in that process, some jobs will be lost (for example, toll booth operators are no longer

needed when toll booths are modernized with cashless, electronic toll booths). Either way, you need to stay on top of the trends in your field by being willing to learn new procedures or software programs. One excellent way to continue learning is to attend industry conferences.

3. **Remain adaptable:** Those with personality types that allow smoother adjustment to sudden change (such as the SP temperament mentioned in Chapter Four) will adjust faster, but all personality types can learn to be more adaptable. Half of the battle is accepting that the only constant is change. The other half is being intentional. Understand the necessity of evolution, and find ways to increase your agility.

4. **Appreciate failure:** There are so many stories and research on the ways that failure helps you grow and enables you to reach greater heights, as long as you don't wallow in self-pity. With each perceived failure, take an inventory of what happened and how you can learn to avoid that pitfall in the future.

5. **Stay curious:** Being curious is a proven way to stay engaged in work and life. Allow yourself time to explore long-held curiosities. Try driving home a new way and see what you discover. Join a new group and see if you click with someone. Change up your routines every so often to encourage novelty and keep your curiosity alive.

6. **Develop a growth mindset:** A growth mindset is optimal for successful career management. It encompasses many of the elements listed above, and it requires the belief in one's ability to change. Carol Dweck has done a wealth of research and writing on the topic of growth mindset.

7. **Create a portfolio career (preferably with multiple streams of income):** There's nothing wrong with being happily employed as a W-2 worker, but it's always a good idea to take charge of your career by exploring passions and engaging in entrepreneurial thinking. If you have something to fall back on financially, it's easier to stay resilient during times of career transition.

8. **Grow and nourish relationships:** The best way to keep your career options fluid is to develop a strong network and stay in touch. Give generously, and remember to ask for help, too, but don't be the person who only calls when she needs something. Try to find supportive professional groups, such as job clubs or a LeanIn circle. The LeanIn website helps you locate a supportive circle near you at https://leanin.org/circles.

9. **Stay positive:** No one likes to be around a sulky person for long periods of time. Find authentic ways to be grateful for what you have and share that happiness. This goes along with the belief in abundance rather than scarcity. If you see your career as a competition, you will only see winners and losers. If you see that there are enough opportunities for everyone, you will look for ways to create opportunities for others and collaborate when possible. What comes around goes around.

10. **Address mental health issues:** However you choose to face your demons, please don't do it alone. Find support in the way of therapy, support groups, education, or self-care, but take control of your mental health. It's hard to have a great career and be your authentic self when you don't feel mentally healthy.

11. **Be okay in the neutral zone:** When going through transition, allow yourself time to process the transition, and seek support from trusted friends and colleagues.

12. **Stay open to planned happenstance:** Have you ever heard of the planned happenstance theory? It was created by Dr. John Krumboltz, who passed away in 2019. He spent much of his life's work on this idea.

    One key point of his theory suggests that stepping out of your comfort zone and exploring curiosities creates opportunities. In the book, *Luck Is No Accident*, he explores the idea that we can create our own luck in careers by taking advantage of unplanned events. As we explore careers by holding informational interviews, researching future possibilities, and seeking out new opportunities, we plant seeds along the way that might come to fruition at the right moment.

He saw indecision as desirable because it provides an opportunity to benefit from unplanned events. As he stated, "So if you are undecided about your future (as indeed every sensible person should be), don't call yourself undecided; call yourself open-minded." The best lesson from his theory is to give some time for planning but also be mindful that things will happen that we can't predict. Adjust plans accordingly and remain open to new ideas.

He also recommends giving yourself credit when it's due. Many times, people attribute their circumstances to pure luck, but if you listen to the person's story closely, you will see times where they took action and remained open to curiosity, which led them in a new and fulfilling direction.

Jody's story—the evolution of a career

After graduating with a bachelor's in religious philosophy from a midwestern school, Jody moved to Washington and earned a certificate in massage therapy after nine months of training. During her education, she held a special interest in acupressure, but she knew she would have to apply her massage credentials to make an income before taking on any more education. Once certified, she landed a job at a resort on Orcas Island. She enjoyed this new job, which offered a generous split of income with the resort, letting each masseuse keep 60% of the income from each session. However, after a year, she became unexpectedly pregnant with her first child.

Jody later had a second child and moved to nearby Lopez Island. She had worked for employers part time while raising her children, but now she wanted to get back to full-time work. There were no massage therapy practices on her island, so entrepreneurship was her next best career option. This offered the bonus aspects of flexibility in scheduling and the ability to earn the full rate. She rented space and started taking on clients. Her massage practice provided a steady income and career satisfaction for many years. But after 20 years of providing body work, she was starting to doubt that her body could handle 20 more years.

Jody took time to reflect on where she was in her career. She still loved the knowledge of the human body, how it functioned, and ways to keep it healthy. She decided to become an acupuncturist to learn more ways to heal others. Realizing she would be able to command a higher rate and have far less wear and tear on her body, she enrolled in acupuncture school. With a combination of her own savings and help from family members, she started her new path. It took three years to earn her master's degree in East Asian medicine and acupuncture. Jody has been practicing now for 12 years and is loving it. She incorporates both manual body work and acupuncture into her practice. She doesn't regret anything, except not furthering her education sooner.

Jody always had a dream of being part of a larger healing center. In 2011, she took on the added role of landlord after moving to a larger facility that provided space for her own practice with additional rooms to sublet to other healthcare professionals. At first, this provided money to offset her costs. After six years, this arrangement provided "free" space to Jody and even brought in $100 a month. And then COVID-19 happened. All tenants were prevented from practicing, though some are slowly coming back. During the pandemic, Jody stopped working, but she kept the leased space. Government subsidies provided funds to help her survive. In July 2020, she returned to her practice.

SUMMARY

- Use the A.S.T.E.R. Career Model anytime you are at a crossroads in your career.

- Seek out support, be kind to yourself, and take time for reflection when you go through each career transition.

- Periodically ask yourself introspective questions about your career path.

"Dig your well before you're thirsty."

ANCIENT CHINESE PROVERB

CHAPTER THIRTEEN

Networking

As someone who cares about career management, most likely you appreciate that networking is an inevitable part of conducting a job search and managing your career well. It's necessary in one form or another to achieve a successful career. It can't be avoided or outsourced. Though you may have assistance with tracking down prospects or knowing when to follow up, ultimately you need to be a key part of this process because networking is personal.

Many people avoid networking because they say they don't enjoy it. However, I find that many people come to enjoy it when they have a more accurate view of what it is. Networking is merely meeting new people and staying in touch with them in a thoughtful way. It's really that simple. Networking is not trying to meet as many people as possible in a short time frame. Nor is it about constantly bragging about yourself and dominating conversations.

You begin networking when you strike up a conversation in the grocery line, when you speak to the other person who came early to the meeting, even at a social party that has nothing to do with your profession. You never know where a conversation can lead. I've seen many examples of a chance conversation with a stranger leading to a job (directly and indirectly), but networking always requires following up.

Women can use intrinsic skills to enhance their networking efforts. As women, we tend to be natural community builders. You often see this take place in workplaces but also schools and community organizing. If you are passionate about a social cause, find a group that meets to address that issue. If you can't find a group, consider creating one. Meeting with others who share a common purpose can also create a supportive system and expand your network in positive ways.

COVID-19 certainly changed some facets of networking, specifically by taking away the ability to meet face-to-face. It can be harder to build a connection with someone virtually, but it can be done. You must pay closer attention to non-verbal language and prepare for technical difficulties. You may need to be more strategic in creating opportunities to see others, since you can't count on naturally crossing paths. Thanks to COVID-19, it can be easier to connect with people who live far from you. The advantage of virtual meetings is the ability to expand your networking to a wider geographic area, without having to incur the cost of travel.

While some methods of networking have changed because of COVID-19, the foundations of networking remain unchanged. You may have to invite someone to a Zoom meeting instead of inviting them to have a cup of coffee, but the basic principles of giving generously and putting in time to develop relationships are still paramount no matter what the avenue for connecting. It still takes effort to reach out to others and follow up with them.

Who is in/should be in my network?

Many clients tell me that they don't have a network, but that's never true. We all know other people, so you need to take an inventory of who you know. If you don't think you know enough people, make a plan to increase the size of your network.

To take stock, think about your network, and, if it's helpful, break them down into subcategories. People may appear listed in more than one category, and that's okay.

People you already know

Social: family, friends, friends of friends, friends of family, people from your local communities (religious, educational, neighborhood, etc.)

Professional: current colleagues, former colleagues, fellow members in professional associations, former bosses, experts in your field

Online connections: Your LinkedIn connections or other social media contacts, people following you on social media, people you are following

Current and former students: Don't forget about others who attended the same schools as you. This will mostly affect college graduates, but even some high schools have serious alumni circles. Generally, people who went to the same school would be willing to help a former classmate (even if you didn't attend at the same time). Use the LinkedIn Alumni Tool to find fellow alumni in your industry. There are multiple ways to access the Alumni Tool, but the easiest is to go to your LinkedIn profile page, and click on the name of the school you attended. Once you land on the school page, click on the tab titled "Alumni." Another way is to log in using this LinkedIn Alumni url at www.linkedin.com/alumni. Please note that for this feature to work, you must have the institution listed under the education section of your profile.

People you want to get to know

It's not who you know but who you can get to know! Think strategically for a moment. Who are the top five people who could accelerate your career if they knew you? These could be experts in your field or influencers with access to an audience. Find out what groups they belong to or if there are events or conferences they are likely to attend or speak at.

Here are five people I would love to get to know:

1) _____

2) _____

3) _____

4) _____

5) _____

Make a plan of action to get on the radar of these folks. This could mean following them on social media (and sharing and commenting on their social media posts). If they host a podcast, listen and share their content. If appropriate, ask to be a future guest.

If you attend an event where they are present, make every effort to shake their hand and let them know how excited you are to meet them. Find out if they are holding any events in your area in the next year, and make a point to attend. Figure out who they know. You might gather this information from their online content or by viewing their contacts/followers, when possible. Sometimes, it's useful to try to get to know one of their contacts, establish trust, and then ask that person to introduce you to the other person.

The levels of a network can vary

Consider how close you are with each connection. It makes sense that you will have degrees of closeness. Usually, we have stronger ties to those we know in more than one way. Some people you will have known for many years and others you will have just met. As you document your network, distinguish how well you know the person, which may change over time. You can color code, create a rating system, or just make a mental note. The main reason to note your level of closeness is so that you don't ask for inappropriate favors. You wouldn't ask someone you just met to help you move, so don't ask a new contact if they can hire you right away.

In *Make Your Contacts Count,* authors Anne Baber and Lynne Waymon offer a six-stage model for categorizing your network (accidents, acquaintances, associates, actors, advocates, and allies). As you might suspect, accidental meetings are the most casual and will usually not produce immediate benefits because you don't know the person well enough to ask for a favor. Allies are the strongest association, and you will have fewer of them. If you click well with someone, your goal should be to grow the relationship to the highest level that makes sense.

Make your network diverse

If you only stick with people you know, you are bound to have a lot of overlap and may never create new connections. Avoid only connecting with people in your geographic area who work in the same industry and are about the same age. A diverse set of connections is your best bet.

I like to say that it's the outer layers of the onion that produce the most success when it comes to job search and networking. The more layers, the greater the potential of your network. The truth is that knowing your mom will not likely directly lead to your next opportunity. However, the person your mom roomed with in college has a daughter whose husband could have an opportunity that leads to your next job. It's the well-known six degrees of separation at play here, but having a diverse network is only as good as the relationships you nurture. So, don't just collect acquaintances. Intentionally try to grow ties with people you enjoy upon first contact.

Realistically, if you really try to diversify, which most people don't, you may encounter others with strongly opposing views. Diversify by seeking out people who are in different fields and other locations, but align with those who have similar values and interests for some harmony. Otherwise, it might be hard to get motivated to grow the relationship.

Places to network

Networking is something you should do across the entire course of your career. Don't make the mistake of only meeting and keeping in touch with others when you are looking for work. Your career goals will guide where you should be networking. When you are in job search mode, it's important to meet new and former connections as much as possible. Specifically for job seekers, there are local workforce offices and community job clubs.

Professionals in all stages of their careers should join and engage with professional associations related to their field. These organizations can provide a wealth of information, from trends in your industry to job postings, and they often have a local chapter that meets on a regular basis. Consider joining your local group first and then possibly the national organization as well. Usually, the local group offers rich networking opportunities, while the larger association offers access to industry resources.

I understand there's not enough money or time in the world to join every association that interests you. Some group memberships can be quite expensive, but you can usually find a lower-priced alternative. For example, joining a local chapter can be less expensive than joining the national organization. You have to be selective. Personally, I could attend events for human resources, career counseling, training, and entrepreneurs, and there are multiple groups meeting the needs of each area.

One trick to get involved without spending too much money is to volunteer to help at events, an especially good idea if you're unemployed. Some organizations are run by volunteers, and some have paid staff. While some places will require you to be a member in order to volunteer, some will not. You need to research the groups you would like to engage with before fully committing to one. I have found that volunteering to cover the registration desk for an in-person group event is an excellent way to network. You get to greet everyone and reference each face to a list of names. The list usually shares the company affiliation, and most times you can attend the event once you've completed registration. At that point, you can strategically walk over to someone you want to know better, and you are now a familiar face since you welcomed them to the event. I have personally tried this tactic and it has worked very well.

Be prepared

Have your introductions ready. This will be easier if you know yourself well. If you are stuck on that, go back to the beginning of this book and review the assessment piece.

I once heard the term "authentically rehearsed" by Ryan Williams during a conference keynote and loved it (keynote, GAD annual conference sponsored by the National Association of Realtors, Portland, OR, July 2018). This phrase captures the idea that it's a good idea to practice saying something if it's important. You want your introductions to come out naturally, but in order to do that it helps to prepare a script. Don't worry that you'll sound like a robot with too much preparation. Worry more that you'll come off as scattered and babbling if you don't.

Networking cards

It's great to have a card you can give as a takeaway after meeting someone. It's an easy reference tool for staying in touch.

If you have a business card for work, that's the obvious choice for you. If you have your own business, whether full time or as a side gig, you should also have business cards for that purpose.

Either way, your cards should share your contact information and be branded with a logo or tagline. It's quite easy these days to get cards made quickly and easily through online services like Vistaprint, https://www.vistaprint.com/. Stores like Staples or Office Depot will sell blank cards you can print on your own printer, or they can design and print them for you.

Systems are key

What will you do with all of those business cards you collect from others? You need to have some process for the cards, besides letting them build up in a pile. Will you sort the hard copies alphabetically? Will you scan them using an app on your phone? With technology there are many solutions. Whatever you choose, stick to it.

It's great to stay in touch with many people if you have enough time, but most of us need to be selective with our time, so you'll need to decide who to focus on. Think about who you most need to stay in touch with and lay out a system to do it. This might mean investing in a customer relationship management tool to notify you when to make a call or the date of someone's birthday. Or create your own system. The idea is to have some way to track who you meet and intentionally follow up.

Your system should track, at minimum, when/where you first met and how often you have spoken/want to speak to the person. The first time you follow up, it's nice to mention when and where you met to refresh the person's memory. After this, it's great to periodically share information relevant to their work or interests. If you are comfortable doing so, you can send the person updates about yourself and inquire how things are going with them.

My techniques

I have created my own contact strategy that I call the 5/5/5. One day a week, usually Monday mornings, I reach out to five former or current clients, five organizations who could hire me, and five colleagues. This provides a nice balance of business development and community support. You could make your own 5/5/5 system to include target organizations for a job search or influencers you'd like to get to know. I am human, so I have fallen short executing this strategy sometimes. At times, I have taken a break from it during holidays or a month in the summertime. However, I've definitely noticed that when I stick to it, more opportunities come my way. If 5/5/5 seems daunting to you, start with a number that seems more manageable. The main point is to make it a consistent part of your weekly routine.

Another technique is to block out time the day or two following an event (for example, a virtual or in-person conference) to reach out to people who interested you. These could be people you met and liked or maybe one of the speakers you heard. So next time you add an event with networking potential to your calendar, at the same time, block off a couple of hours the next possible day for follow up activities. Most people don't follow-up at all, but even fewer do it shortly after the event. You will stand out if you do this.

What is a CRM? A Customer Relationship Management (CRM) system is an electronic tool to help you store and track contact information. They can vary greatly in their level of sophistication. Some are basic and free (for example, creating an Excel spreadsheet) and others are complex and expensive (think Salesforce or Infusionsoft). They have a variety of capabilities from scheduling clients to sending invoices and everything in between. It's important to find one that meets your specific needs. Do research on each product and read reviews from current/past users. Most are designed for salespeople and businesses, but I know of some that are designed specifically for therapists (Therapynotes at https://www.therapynotes.com/or SimplePractice at https://www.simplepractice.com/) or career coaches (CoachesConsole at https://coachesconsole.com/). Obviously, the more names you have and the bigger your business, the more likely you are to need a higher level system.

Jibberjobber found at https://www.jibberjobber.com/login.php is a useful CRM designed uniquely for job seekers. It offers the ability to store your resume, prepare for interviews, track expenses and save job postings. Like many online services, there are free and paid subscriptions. Jason Alba, the company's founder, created this tool after being laid off from a tech job. He became tired of using an Excel spreadsheet and wanted to create something with his IT know-how that could benefit other job seekers.

Scripts

You might think of your script as a branding statement or an elevator pitch. No matter what you call it, you should have a few scripts spelled out to help you with your networking. You might have a version for within your company and one for those outside of the organization (your internal version may include acronyms and jargon known at your company). You could have a shorter version (for when you have to stand up briefly to introduce yourself) and a longer version (for a one-to-one meeting). It's likely that the main theme of your content will not change that much; you are just tweaking it slightly to adjust to each situation. The examples below can provide a starting point to create your own scripts.

Words for casually meeting someone new at an in-person event:

"It's nice to meet you _____ (repeat their name to help you remember it). I'm Paula, and I came to this event today to learn/listen/see about _____. What brought you here today?"

Words for a networking event where you have to give a brief introduction:

"Hello, everyone. I'm excited to be here and thank you for the opportunity to attend today. My name is Paula Brand, and I run Brand Career Management, a full-service career coaching business. My passion is helping mid-career to executive women succeed in their careers."

In the new reality of our highly virtual world, you may have these scripts pre-typed so that you can easily add them into a chat box during a Zoom meeting.

For more ideas on scripting, check out *100 Conversations for Career Success* by Laura Labovich and Miriam Salpeter. This is an excellent resource for all types of scripts related to networking and job search. It offers 15 chapters of scripts for every career situation imaginable.

Six networking principles for success

Do it now: As the quote at the beginning of this chapter states, dig your well before you're thirsty! Don't wait until you need your network. Make some form of networking a regular habit, even if it's just meeting with a different person each month for lunch. Harvey Mackay has written an excellent book on networking, and the title may sound familiar: *Dig Your Well Before You're Thirsty.*

Give and take: Networking should be a two-way street of give and take over time. It's always best to give before asking for something. Adam Grant's book *Give and Take* explains that the most effective networkers give AND take. The less effective people either take too much (these folks generally have a reputation for only making contact when they need something) or give too much (never making any requests, even when it's very appropriate to do so). It's great to give, but you do need to set boundaries. If you don't, some folks will take advantage of your generosity. When people give too much, they often neglect their own needs. I firmly believe in karma and have seen it play out many times. The old saying, "What comes around, goes around" is often at play with networking. So, don't be afraid to ask for help when needed, and always think about how you can help others. This could mean sharing information, connecting two people you know, or just doing something nice for someone.

With networking, there is an unspoken system of credits and withdrawals. While you don't need to keep a detailed account of favors given and received, you should have some sense of balance and strive for reciprocity. You might do something nice for someone knowing you may ask them for a favor down the road. Some people think this is too manipulative. I say, "It's strategic." As long as you are both giving and receiving with a person over the long term, you should maintain good relations.

Follow up and think ahead: Once you meet someone you enjoyed getting to know, make a point to let them know you are glad your paths crossed. This is a great first step in developing an accidental meeting into a new relationship. Stay in touch through email, social media, or a coffee, if it's possible. Be sure to attend conferences and look for opportunities to reconnect later on. Reach out to colleagues who might be registered for an event and see if they plan to go. If they are, suggest that you might connect during the event. I always do this, and I never regret it. Or if I know I am going to a new location, I check to see if there are other career professionals I might want to get to know there.

Be present: When you are speaking to someone, take time to slow down and listen carefully. Minimize distractions. Maintain eye contact to display your focus. Don't keep looking at your phone. It will give the impression that you are not very interested in the person or the conversation. We often forget people's names when we first meet because we are not fully present. Asking questions and listening carefully to the answers can help keep you in the moment.

Remember names: When you first hear a name, make an association in your brain. If you know someone with the same name, you could even say out loud, "My sister's name is Lisa." Or if it's a name like Violet, you could associate it with the flower or the color. Try to repeat the name as soon as possible and use it during the conversation to move it into long-term memory. One word of caution: Don't use the name excessively. This can feel insincere, strange, or like you are a salesperson.

Make sure you say the name correctly—check if needed. Ask them to say their name so you can hear it pronounced correctly. If attending an in-person meeting, look at their name tag. If attending a virtual meeting, look to see what name is displaying for the attendee. Seeing and hearing the name helps retention, rather than only using one modality. Sometimes, even visualizing the name on their forehead can work.

Remember people's birthdays and big milestones: This will usually endear people to you because it shows you care enough to keep them in mind. It can also show you were listening to them and you heard them. For example, if you meet someone at a networking event and find out that the next month they are taking an exam for a professional credential, they will be quite impressed if you follow up after one month to ask how it turned out. This is where a CRM can be very helpful as it's not realistic to remember many birthdays of acquaintances. Most CRM systems allow you to record birthdays (and will send you reminders) and notes (i.e., Paula's daughter graduates high school next year).

Why people don't network more

Below are some of the excuses I hear about why people don't network more often. They say:

"I don't want to bother others."

"Networking is fake."

"I'm an introvert so I'm not good at it."

"I don't think people will say yes to my request to meet up."

"I don't have the time." (This may be a legitimate reason, but you need to find ways to make time because it is such an important activity.)

"I don't like to talk about myself."

Let's refute each of these misperceptions one by one.

"I don't want to bother others."

In group training, I often ask people to raise their hands if they would be willing to speak with someone else about the work they do. Each time, almost everyone sends up a hand. People generally underestimate how much others are willing to help them with careers and job search. Research by Francis Flynn and Vanessa Lake of Columbia University suggested that people grossly underestimate how much others are willing to help. I realize not every person you ask will work out, but if you ask 10 people, you should find at least three who are willing and able to help at that moment.

"Networking is fake."

It's only fake if you are, so be authentic. Try to create sincere curiosity to know more about what others are up to. Usually, people who think that networking is fake also picture someone coming into a room and trying to hand out as many business cards as possible, but that's not networking. That is a person who wants to rush through the process of meeting people and in doing so, really doesn't connect with anyone.

This is the biggest myth about networking. Meeting as many people in the room as possible should never be your goal. There are many reasons why. Besides the fact that trying to meet everyone is unrealistic, it can also be a waste of time. You want to zero in on a few people and have some quality conversations to establish a relationship that may grow over time.

"I'm an introvert so I'm not good at it."

There is so much information explaining how introverts can be very adept at networking by employing their strengths of listening and thoughtful engagement. In fact, some would say these strengths make introverts more effective than extroverts when it comes to networking because extroverts are more likely to interrupt, dominate conversations, and listen poorly.

If you feel like more of an introvert (or even if you don't), there are some things you can do to ease the stress of networking:

1) Strive for one-to-one conversation. Introverts generally fare better in more intimate interactions so rather than approaching a group of people already speaking, why not find a person in the room who is standing alone? With networking, one deep conversation is better than 20 shallow ones.

2) Do your homework. When possible, try to find out who is on the guest list for an event. Ask the coordinator if this information is available or offer to help with the check-in process.

This way, you'll see each person as they enter the event (virtual or in-person) and be able to connect each face with a name.

If the guest list has been made available, look up some of the attendees on LinkedIn to see what you can find out about where they went to school or what they do. This can be especially helpful if you are trying to meet someone from a specific organization.

3) Have questions ready to ask others so you can turn the conversation over to them. People love to talk about themselves, so give them a reason to do so.

Recommended reading

Quiet! The Power of Introverts in a World That Can't Stop Talking by Susan Cain

The Introverts, Complete Career Guide: From Landing a Job, Surviving, Thriving, and Moving on Up by Jane Finkle

Hiding in the Bathroom: How to Get Out There When You'd Rather Stay Home by Morra Aarons-Mele

"I don't think people will say yes to my request to meet up."

Assume the best and think positively. You are not asking to borrow money. You are simply asking someone to speak with you for a short period of time. No one likes rejection, and you will face some of that when trying to meet new people. You'll click with some better than others—and that's okay. Once you try it a few times and see success, you will gain confidence initiating and conducting conversations with people you didn't know before. Building this skill will also make you more comfortable with job interviews.

"I don't have the time."

I think by far the hardest part of networking for most people is making the time to do it. Our world is a very busy one these days, so it's not easy, but relationships won't grow if you don't stay in communication. Therefore, you need to be very intentional about staying in touch with others or it won't happen.

Networking is one of those things that is important but will rarely be urgent. You must make time for it. Figure out which methods work best for your style and schedule (for example, meeting for coffee/lunch, calling people, reaching out on social media, and so on). Then, set out a plan covering how often you will reach out, to how many people, and how you will measure success (for example, to meet two new people a month, to stay in touch with current contacts by emailing every quarter, etc.).

"I don't like to talk about myself"

I've met people from many cultures and worked with many people born in the U.S. To date, I have yet to meet someone who says they are comfortable talking about their accomplishments. This will probably always be challenging, but you must implement strategies to make it easier. If you can't share your successes, how can you add value or show how you are unique? Others cannot magically know these things. If they don't know your strengths and dreams, it's hard for them to direct appropriate opportunities your way to help you achieve your goals.

One strategy is to have a sentence or two prepared ahead to reply to, "What do you do?" Your answer could explain what you do and why it matters. It could also share a big goal you are working toward or something you love to do in your spare time. Any of these could be a starting point to offer some information about yourself to begin a conversation. Then, you can have a few questions prepared to ask others to turn the conversation away from yourself. You could ask the common question, "What do you do?" Or you could make it more interesting by asking, "What is something that's really important to you?"

Some people see talking about oneself as bragging, so let's address this here. At some point, you may want to share some accomplishments you've made because they are relevant to the conversation at hand, so you'll need to learn how to share good things you've done without feeling uncomfortable. There is a great book that walks you through this process in depth. The author takes you through steps to build stories from your life that you can work into conversations to share your talents in a natural way. She suggests creating a "brag bag" of brag bites and "bragalogues" to have in your back pocket for the right moment. Telling your stories allows you to showcase your strengths with enthusiasm and conviction. Below are some questions to consider as you prepare things you might say. Take a minute to jot some ideas down and come back later to flesh them out.

Recommended reading

BRAG! The Art of Tooting Your Own Horn Without Blowing It by Peggy Klaus

What are some interesting or challenging things you have done in your lifetime?

If you have done something unusual (once or as a hobby), like scuba diving or skydiving, most people will remember that about you. In 2003, I traveled across the Asian Pacific Rim with my husband for one year. This trip fascinates people, and they always want to hear more. In fact, I've come to appreciate that it's the most interesting thing about me. I used to never bring it up because it was in the past, it didn't tie to my work, and I didn't want to sound pretentious. Now, I share it when it makes sense, and it also ties to the personal brand I've built of being a global person. Speaking about it more often has made me more comfortable sharing it. Also, it has attracted other global-minded people to me and makes people from other cultures feel more comfortable around me. Later on, it helped position me to land a contractual gig at the World Bank.

What are you most proud of in your career to date?

Usually, if you are proud of it, it was a success and drew upon your strengths, so this can be a great place to begin documenting your repertoire of stories to share. It's also sometimes asked in an interview, so thinking about it beforehand will make your presentation stronger.

What is something you would like to see happen in the next few years?

This can be scary to share, and it's not appropriate for every situation, but it's a great way to build support and resources that can help you reach your future goals. You'll be surprised how many people can help you if they know what you are reaching for.

Madeline's networking story

Madeline illustrates a great example of asking for and receiving help in a virtual setting. She is a member of an online community for instructional designers called Pedago.me. She was preparing an interview that required her to create a video explaining how she would handle a case study. The scenario involved preparing for the first meeting with a professor to explain what digital tools she would use to modernize the course material. Madeline had never done this type of work before, so she went on Pedago.me to ask for help. In one of the chat channels, she asked how one might help an art professor take her drawing class online. Three people responded generously with helpful information. As a result, not only did Madeline learn about document cameras, which was a vital tool for completing the assignment, she also secured an additional job interview at a local community college.

SUMMARY

- Networking is talking to others and staying in touch with people you enjoy, so you grow the relationship.

- Map out your network to see how large it is and where it is stronger or weaker. Set a strategy to maintain strong relationships and firm up weaker ties.

- There are many places to network. Make a list of places and organizations that make sense for your networking activities.

- Be prepared (have tools, systems, and scripts in place to make things easier).

- Follow the six strategies for successful networking (start now, give and take, remember names and milestones, follow up, think ahead, and be present).

- There are many excuses people make to avoid networking. Don't fall prey to them if you care about your career.

ACTIVITIES

In addition to the exercises in the chapter, try some of these activities individually or with a group. If you are in a group, give a few of these for homework and have people report back on results.

1) Find two organizations in your area that focus on the same things you do and attend one of their events.

2) Go on LinkedIn and search for others in your industry who also attended the same school.

3) Make a record of the number of people in your network. Set a goal to increase the number of people in your professional network within a year by a total or percentage (shorter time frame if in job search).

4) Set a goal for meeting new people. For example, you might say, "I will meet two new people each month for six months." In the seventh month, evaluate which people you connected well with and which might help you find new opportunities. For those you want to develop a relationship with, plan a way to touch base three times in the next year and see what happens.

5) Think about an expert or influencer in your field who you would like to get to know (or who you think you could help in some way). Find them on social media and follow or connect with them, if possible. Schedule time to visit their page three times in the next six months and make a point to comment, like, and/or share some of their content.

6) See if any influencers/experts live nearby and ask to take them to coffee or lunch. If they are a traveling performer/speaker, see if they might be coming to your area in the future.

7) Set aside an hour to assess your "pile of cards," and think about how you want to organize them, assess the amount of time it will take, and schedule that amount of time on your calendar.

Epilogue

We've covered a lot of ground in this book. If you've worked your way through each chapter, you've done a lot of work on discovering or rediscovering your V.I.N.E.S. and reached (or are on your way to reaching) the next phase of your career. Once done, I hope you take the time to breathe and appreciate what you've achieved. Enjoy your new path for the time it serves you, and don't be afraid to create new directions later on.

When you want to make another career change or feel stuck, go through the A.S.T.E.R. Career Model process again. It is a method that can be used over and over no matter how the workforce changes because knowing yourself well is always the best place to begin a career transition or job search. And while technology will continue to disrupt the job search process, networking will always be the best way to find a job.

No matter what your career, my sincere hope is that you gained clarity for moving it forward after reading this book. If it worked for you, please share your story with me. I'd love to hear from you paula@brandcareer-management.com.

Acknowledgements

Thanks to my mom and dad!

My mom taught me what it means to be a strong, dedicated, involved woman and that it's never too late to start your professional career.

By creating a successful executive recruitment business from scratch, my dad showed me that entrepreneurship is a viable path and how satisfying it can be to see people get hired.

To my siblings for their support and specifically to Lisa for providing my first voice of encouragement after reading a rough draft of the first few chapters. To my brother Stephen, I wish you were here to read this.

To all of my friends and family who kept asking me about my progress on this book and listened when I needed a friendly ear.

To clients who allowed me into their lives so I could learn from them. All of those experiences helped me write this book.

To colleagues who supported me by giving feedback, brainstorming ideas, and encouraging me along the way, especially Gloria Monick, Karla Wynn, and Barry Davis.

To authors who inspired me. Some were asked to be a source of support and accountability, including Shahrzad Arasteh, Sharon Armstrong, William Arruda, Dorie Clark, Marcia Hall, Hannah Morgan, Elisabeth Sanders, and Ilana Tolpin Levitt. Thanks to Jason Alba for planting the seed for this book. Thanks to each of you for being a role model in some way.

To everyone who read a version of a rough draft and provided feedback, including my mom, Laurie Nederveen, Karen Chopra, Sabira Vohra, and Dennis Weeks. Also, a big thanks to Maggie Rogers for providing encouragement, proofreading, and excellent stylistic advice over Zoom. To the Get It Done publishing team for their help in making this book a reality.

To everyone who reads this book. Thank you for taking the time to do so. If you have feedback to share, please write me at paula@paulabrand.com.

And of course, to my amazing husband who always provides strength and has fully supported me through this entire endeavor.

About The Author

Paula Battalia Brand is the founder of Brand Career Management, a global career coach, and a LinkedIn expert. She was born and raised in a suburb of New York City, having first picked up the importance of job search skills and resume development from her father, a trailblazer in the world of executive recruiting firms. She holds a master's degree in organizational/industrial psychology and has enjoyed a variety of roles in human resources, workforce development, and career advising. An inspirational leader, Paula is passionate about helping women succeed in their careers. She values working with mid-career and executive women to empower them on their professional journey.

Paula and her husband have called Maryland their home for many years while traveling the world, expanding their knowledge of people and places.

Find out more about Paula at paulabrand.com and access bonus resources at purple-parachute.com/bonus.

Bibliography

Aarons-Mele, Morra. *Hiding in the Bathroom: How to Get Out There When You'd Rather Stay Home*. New York, NY: Dey Street Books, 2018.

Arasteh, Shahrzad. *Nourish Your Career: Recipes to Help You Thrive in Your Work and Life*. (self-pub., 2013).

Arruda, William. *Digital You: Personal Branding in the Virtual Age*. Alexandria, VA: Atd Press, 2019.

Arruda, William and Kirsten Dixson. *Career Disinction: Stand Out by Building Your Brand*. Hoboken, NJ: Wiley, 2007.

Babcock, Linda and Sara Laschever. *Women Don't Ask: Negotiation and the Gender Divide*. Princeton, NY: Princeton University Press, 2021

Baber, Anne and Lynne Waymon. *Make Your Contacts Count: Networking Know-How for Business and Career Success*. 2nd Ed. New York, NY: AMACOM, 2007.

Bennett, Jessica. *Feminist Fight Club: A Survival Manual for a Sexist Workplace*. New York, NY: Harper Wave, 2017.

Bolles, Richard N. and Katharine Brooks. *What Color Is Your Parachute?* Berkeley, CA: Ten Speed Press, 2021.

"Bridges Transition Model." n.d. William Bridges Associates. Accessed April 24, 2022. https://wmbridges.com/about/what-is-transition/

Cain, Susan. *Quiet: The Power of Introverts in a World That Can't Stop Talking*. New York, NY: Crown, 2013.

Careerblast.TV. "Personal Brand Survey." n.d. Accessed May 25, 2022. https://careerblast.tv/personal-branding-products/360reach-personal-branding-survey/

Clark, Dorie. *Entrepreneurial You: Monetize Your Expertise, Create Multiple Income Streams, and Thrive.* Brighton, MA: Harvard Business Review Press, 2017.

Clark, Dorie. *The Long Game: How to Be a Long-Term Thinker in a Short-Term World.* Brighton, MA: Harvard Business Review Press, 2021.

Clark, Dorie. *Reinventing You: Define Your Brand, Imagine Your Future.* Brighton, MA: Harvard Business Review Press, 2013.

Clark, Dorie. *Stand Out: How to Find Your Breakthrough Idea and Build a Following Around It.* New York, NY: Portfolio, 2015.

Covey, Stephen. *The 7 Habits of Highly Effective People.* 30th Anniversary Edition. New York, NY: Simon & Schuster, 2020.

Dweck, Carol. *Mindset: The New Psychology of Success.* New York, NY: Ballantine Books, 2007.

Enelow, Wendy and Louise Kursmark. *Modernize Your Resume: Get Noticed... Get Hired.* 2nd Ed. Coleman Falls, VA: Emerald Career Publishing, 2019.

Enelow, Wendy and Louise Kursmark. *The Best Keywords for Resumes, Letters, and Interviews: Powerful Words and Phrases for Landing Great Jobs!* Santa Clarita, CA: Impact Publishing, 2016.

eParachute.com. "Online Career Exploration for Work You Love – Inspired by *What Color Is Your Parachute?* – Eparachute." 2016. https://eparachute.com/

Finkle, Jane. *The Introverts, Complete Career Guide: From Landing a Job, to Surviving, Thriving, and Moving on Up.* Newburyport, MA: Wesier, 2019.

Flynn, Francis and Veronica Lake "If You Need Help, Just Ask: Underestimating Compliance with Direct Requests for Help." *Journal of Personality and Social Psychology,* 95(1), (2008): 128–143, https://doi.org/10.1037/0022-3514.95.1.128

Gallup.com. "Live Your Best Life Using Your Strengths." 2019. https://www.gallup.com/cliftonstrengths/en/252137/home.aspx

Gerber, Michael E. *The E Myth Revisited: Why Most Small Businesses Don't Work and What to Do About It.* 1st Ed. New York, NY: HarperBusiness, 1995.

Gilkey, Charlie. *Start Finishing: How to Go from Idea to Done.* Louisville, CO: Sounds True, 2019.

Godin, Seth. *This Is Marketing: You Can't Be Seen Until You Learn to See.* New York, NY: Portfolio, 2018.

Grant, Adam. *Give and Take: A Revolutionary Approach to Success.* New York, NY: Viking, 2013.

Indeed Editorial Team. "How to Use the Car Interview Method." n.d. Indeed Career Guide. Accessed May 31, 2022. https://www.indeed.com/career-advice/interviewing/car-interview-method

Indeed Editorial Team. "What is a Returnship? Benefits of Return-to-Work Programs." n.d. Indeed Career Guide. Accessed May 21, 2022. https://www.indeed.com/career-advice/finding-a-job/returnship

IResearchNet.com. "Holland's Theory of Vocational Choice." n.d. Accessed March 23, 2015. https://career.iresearchnet.com/career-development/hollands-theory-of-vocational-choice/#google_vignette

Joseph, Jenny and Lydia Coventry. *Warning: When I Am an Old Woman I Shall Wear Purple.* London: Souvenir Press, 2021.

Keirsey.com. "The Four Temperaments." 2019. https://keirsey.com/temperament-overview/

Klaus, Peggy. *BRAG! The Art of Tooting Your Own Horn Without Blowing It.* New York, NY: Warner Business Books, 2004.

Krumboltz, John and Al Levin. *Luck is No Accident: Making the Most of Happenstance in Your Life and Career.* 2nd Ed. Manassas, VA: Impact, 2010.

Labovich, Laura and Miriam Salpeter. *100 Conversations for Career Success: Learn to Network, Cold Call, and Tweet Your Way to Your Dream Job.* New York, NY: Learning Express, 2012.

Levitt, Ilana Tolpin. *What's Mom Still Got to Do with It? Breathe New Life into Your Career by Understanding Your Mother-Daughter Relationship.* (self-pub., 2017).

Litzinger, Karen. *Help Wanted: An A to Z Guide to Cope with the Ups and Downs of the Job Search.* Pittsburgh, PA: Career Spirit Press, 2021.

Mackay, Harvey. *Dig Your Well Before You're Thirsty. The Only Networking Book You'll Ever Need.* Sydney, Australia: Currency, 1999.

Marcusbuckingham.com. "The Gift of Standout." n.d. Accessed May 25, 2022. https://www.marcusbuckingham.com/

Markman, Art. *Bring Your Brain to Work: Using Cognitive Science to Get a Job, Do It Well, and Advance Your Career.* Brighton, MA: Harvard Business Review Press, 2019.

McDonald, Jason. *The Marketing Book: A Marketing Plan for Your Business Made Easy via Think / Do / Measure.* San Jose, CA: J M Internet Group, 2018.

Miller, Lee E. and Jessica Miller. *A Woman's Guide to Successful Negotiating: How to Convince, Collaborate, & Create Your Way to Agreement.* New York, NY: McGraw-Hill, 2002.

National Career Development Association (NCDA). "2015 NCDA Code of Ethics." Glossary of Terms. Accessed May 21, 2022. https://www.ncda.org/aws/NCDA/asset_manager/get_file/3395

Novorésumé.com. "101 Career Paths for Every Personality [2022 Guide]." n.d. Career Blog. Accessed May 25, 2022. https://novoresume.com/career-blog/career-paths-for-every-personality

Port, Michael. *Book Yourself Solid: The Fastest, Easiest, and Most Reliable System for Getting More Clients Than You Can Handle Even if You Hate Marketing and Selling.* 3rd Ed. Hoboken, NJ: Wiley, 2017.

Rinne, April. "Why You Should Build a "Career Portfolio" (Not a "Career Path")." Harvard Business Review. October 13, 2021. https://hbr.org/2021/10/why-you-should-build-a-career-portfolio-not-a-career-path#:~:text=At%20the%20heart%20of%20it,finally%20enter%20its%20prime%20today.

Schlossberg, Nancy K., Elinor B Waters, and Jane Goodman. *Counseling Adults in Transition: Linking Practice with Theory.* 2nd Ed. New York, NY: Springer Publishing Company, 1995.

SHIFT. Midternship™ is trademarked by SHIFT. https://shiftonline.org/ Minneapolis, MN.

Permission granted by Susan Krautbauer. (The definition of midternship has been removed from the SHIFT website when accessed on May 11, 2022.)

TalentLyft.com. "What is Hidden Job Market?" n.d. Recruiting and Hiring Resources. Accessed May 21, 2022. https://www.talentlyft.com/en/resources/what-is-hidden-job-market

Thomas, Rachel. "Women Shoulder Most of the Extra Work Because of COVID-19." LeanIn. April 4, 2020. https://leanin.org/article/women-shoulder-most-of-the-extra-work-because-of-covid-19

Tieger, Paul, Barbara Barron-Tieger, and Kelly Tieger. *Do What You Are: Discover the Perfect Career for You Through the Secrets of Personality Type.* Brunswick, Victoria: Scribe Publications Pty Ltd., 2018.

U.S. Department of Labor. "O*NET Online." n.d. Accessed May 25, 2022. https://www.onetonline.org/

U.S. Department of Labor. "What do you want to do for a living?" n.d. Accessed May 25, 2022. https://www.mynextmove.org/

Index

www.ingramcontent.com/pod-product-compliance
Lightning Source LLC
Chambersburg PA
CBHW071149130626
46553CB00004B/1588